The Secrets of the Great MINDS

Sankhadeep Dutta

BlueRoseONE.com
Stories Matter
New Delhi • London

BLUEROSE PUBLISHERS
India | U.K.

For permissions requests or inquiries regarding this publication, please contact:

BLUEROSE PUBLISHERS
www.BlueRoseONE.com
info@bluerosepublishers.com
+91 8882 898 898
+4407342408967

ISBN: 978-93-7139-743-8

Cover Design: Aman Sharma
Typesetting: Pooja Sharma

First Edition: August 2025

CONTENTS

1. HOW TO NEVER HAVE A WEAK MIND

- Witness Your Truth
- Recognize Emotional Triggers
- Break the Cycle of Negative Reactions
- Cultivate Self-Compassion

1. HOW TO NEVER HAVE A WEAK MINDSET

Everyone wants to appear confident, charismatic, and in control. We all seek respect, admiration, and to be taken seriously. But have you ever paused to consider where that magnetic presence truly comes from? The difference between someone who naturally attracts others and someone who fades into the background often begins with one powerful factor: **mindset.** It's how you think—about yourself, about others, and about the world—that ultimately shapes the way you show up and the impact you leave behind.

By the end of this chapter, you may realize that the way you once viewed weakness, doubt, and inner struggle has transformed. What once felt like a limitation may now appear as an opportunity to build strength—and your mindset may be sharper, tougher, and far more powerful than when you began.

We'll explore the core foundations to appear confident, charismatic and In control—so you can begin cultivating a mindset that stays steady no matter the situation. Even if you've felt emotionally fragile, easily overwhelmed, or prone to overthinking, know this: a powerful, unshakable mindset isn't something you're born with—it's something anyone can build. And that includes you.

WITNESS YOUR TRUTH

Have you ever noticed how, in moments of silence, we often become aware of something deeper within ourselves—a subtle feeling, a quiet thought, or an emotion that lingers just beneath the surface? This act of simply observing what is happening inside us, without trying to change it or push it away, is the beginning of witnessing your truth. Long before we learn to speak or act, we develop the capacity to be aware of our own inner world, and this awareness is the foundation of genuine connection with ourselves.

Many people believe that understanding themselves comes only through action or words, but the deepest form of self-knowledge begins with mindful presence—being fully awake to what is real in the moment. To witness your truth means to hold your thoughts and feelings with acceptance, as if you were gently watching a river flow, without trying to stop or redirect it. This simple but profound practice allows you to step beyond distractions and conditioning, helping you build a strong, authentic mind that responds rather than reacts.

By learning this, you create a space where clarity, peace, and true strength can grow—anchoring you firmly in who you really are.

There are moments in life that arrive without warning—an unexpected confrontation, a job interview you didn't prepare for, someone questioning your worth, or even a deep silence in a crowded room that suddenly makes you feel exposed. In these moments, many people panic. They shrink. Their minds scatter in a thousand directions. What's really happening here isn't just fear—it's a disconnection from their own truth.

To never have a weak mind, the first and most powerful step is this: learn to witness your truth in real time.

What does that mean? It means building the inner muscle to observe yourself—not judge, not react, but observe—especially when your instincts want to run or defend. This witnessing is your anchor. It keeps you grounded when your emotions would rather throw you off balance.

Imagine you're in a meeting and someone disagrees strongly with your idea. A fragile mind will immediately start doubting itself: "Did I say something stupid? Should I apologize? Maybe I'm not good enough." But a strong mind—one trained to witness its truth—pauses. It hears the disagreement, acknowledges the emotion rising in the body, and instead of reacting, it chooses a calm response rooted in clarity, not insecurity.

Witnessing your truth is not only about confidence. It's also about knowing where you stand, even when no one else agrees with you. It's about being honest with yourself in moments of internal chaos.

When your heartbeat races and your throat tightens, you don't pretend it's not happening—you breathe through it, and say to yourself, "This is fear, but it doesn't own me. I see it. I'm still here."

The truth is, most of us were never taught how to stay present when discomfort enters the room. We were taught to perform, to please, to flee, or to fight. But none of those reactions build a strong mind. A strong mind is not built through avoidance or aggression—it is built through awareness and witnessing.

Start watching yourself more closely—not with criticism, but with compassion. Notice when you get reactive. Notice when you fake a smile, when you agree just to avoid conflict, when you pretend you're okay but feel like breaking inside. Each of those moments is not weakness—they are invitations.

Invitations to witness your truth more deeply. And with that awareness, comes power. The kind of power that cannot be shaken by anyone's opinion.

This practice doesn't just help you escape negative feelings—it strengthens your confidence and mental clarity. In fact, there is scientific evidence supporting this approach

Using 'witness your truth' techniques is less about doing something completely new and more about consciously strengthening what you may already be doing on a subconscious level. This process must become natural—something you embody, not just something you try when things get tough. It's about becoming deeply aware of your internal reactions and choosing to respond, not just react.* lets look into small examples-

"Strength isn't about being unbreakable—it's about being unafraid to see yourself clearly. The moment you witness your truth without resistance, fear loses its grip, and leadership begins from within."

RECOGNIZE EMOTIONAL TRIGGERS

Mark Twain once said, "You can't depend on your eyes when your imagination is out of focus." The same goes for emotions. One of the biggest blocks to writing — and success in general — isn't a lack of ideas, talent, or time. It's getting hijacked by our own emotional triggers. The feelings we don't manage end up managing us.

Strong minds know this. They don't ignore emotions — they understand them. Especially the ones that creep in quietly: frustration, envy, fear of judgment, imposter syndrome.

Learning to recognise these triggers — and more importantly, not react blindly to them

— is a key mental skill of every successful author, speaker, or creator.

Psychologist Dr. Susan David explains this through a concept called emotional agility — the ability to experience emotions with curiosity, courage, and clarity. In other words, don't suppress them, don't obey them. Simply notice them, name them, and then choose your response.

Emotional awareness begins with observation. Notice what changes. A slight shift in tone. A break in rhythm. A delay in response. These are not random—they are emotional cues. Most triggers come from three places:

Not feeling understood Feeling dismissed Feeling controlled

When working with driven individuals, recognising these triggers is not optional—it is essential. Because drive does not mean someone is unshakable. It simply means they're less likely to show when they are shaken. The goal is not to manage their reactions, but to understand what caused them. You don't need to fix feelings—just notice them. That alone creates space for trust. And trust is the only ground where driven people truly open up.

Let us take a closer look at emotional triggers, not as obstacles, but as signals that reveal the half story. . Have you observed how sometimes a conversation with a driven person suddenly shifts, as if something invisible has been touched? This is exactly what happens when emotional triggers come into play. They do not always announce themselves loudly; more often, they appear in quiet ways—through resistance, silence, or defensiveness. The challenge is that many of us fail to recognise these moments for what they are and instead misinterpret the response as stubbornness or disengagement. Emotional triggers are rooted in past experiences—times when someone felt unheard, disrespected, or powerless. These experiences create patterns, and when similar situations arise, the emotional trigger activates automatically. For strong individuals who often carry a strong exterior, these triggers may not show openly, but their effect is just as real

A weak mind rushes to defend, justify, or shut down when discomfort arises. But a strong mind—one rooted in clarity—knows how to recognize before it , Think about Andy Dufresne from The Shawshank Redemption. Locked away in a harsh prison, wrongly convicted, facing daily injustice and cruelty, most would have let anger, fear, or despair break them down. But Andy's strength wasn't in ignoring his emotions—it was in witnessing them without letting them control him.

When the walls closed in and his world felt like it was collapsing, Andy didn't lash out or give in to bitterness. Instead, he acknowledged his pain quietly, holding onto his truth deep inside. That calm awareness gave him the power to choose his actions carefully, to plan patiently, and to build hope when everything seemed lost.

Andy's mastery over his emotional triggers didn't come from force or denial, but from a deep inner strength—the kind that waits, observes, and acts with purpose. His story reminds us that **a strong mind** doesn't react hastily in the face of hardship; it listens, learns, and responds with unshakable resilience.

Here are some secrets for winning over emotional triggers—not by suppressing them, but by mastering them with clarity and strength:

1. **Label the Feeling, Don't Become It**

When an emotional wave hits—shame, anger, jealousy—name it with honesty. "This is frustration," or "This is fear." That simple act creates distance between you and the emotion. You're no longer drowning in it—you're observing it from the shore. Awareness is power.

2. **Track the Pattern, Not Just the Moment**

Triggers rarely appear in isolation. Look back—where else did this feeling show up? Is it tied to childhood rejection? Past failures? A need for approval? When you see the pattern, you stop being a slave to the moment. You begin to rewrite your inner script.

3. Regulate Before You Respond

The strongest minds don't speak from a storm. They breathe, step back, and wait for the dust to settle. A calm nervous system leads to a clear voice. Whether it's three breaths or thirty minutes—your best reaction often begins with a pause.

4. Use Triggers as Insight, Not Instruction

A trigger might feel like a command ("lash out," "shut down," "prove your worth"), but it's actually a message. Learn to ask: "What is this trying to show me?" Strong minds don't obey their emotions—they learn from them.

5. Redirect the Energy

Instead of letting a trigger spiral you into overthinking or self-blame, channel that emotional surge into action—write, move, create. Emotional energy doesn't have to destroy; it can also fuel clarity, discipline, and transformation.

"True strength lies not in resisting emotions, but in welcoming them as guides that deepen our understanding and light the path to mindful action."

BREAKING THE NEGATIVE PATTERNS

Are you one of those people who get affected deeply by someone else's negative reaction?

It's a question that touches a universal experience. We all face moments when someone's anger, criticism, or coldness feels like a weight pressing down on us. Negative emotions—from others or from within ourselves—have a remarkable power to unsettle our minds and shake our confidence.

The key is not to banish negative emotions but to meet them with awareness. When you pause and witness these feelings rise, you create a space between the emotion and your response—a space where true freedom begins. Instead of being swept away by anger, sadness, or anxiety, you become the observer. You see them clearly, without judgment, without resistance.

The negative effect? A cycle that repeats itself: negative emotion leads to negative thought, which leads to negative action, which then feeds back into the emotion. Breaking free from this cycle requires conscious awareness—a willingness to witness these emotions honestly and without shame.

Only then can the mind regain its strength. By acknowledging negative emotions as natural and temporary experiences—not defining truths—we create space to respond with clarity, courage, and resilience. This shift transforms the mindset from fragile and reactive into one that is grounded, adaptable, and strong.

If negative thoughts left unexamined, these repeated emotional responses start rewiring your inner world. You begin to expect hurt, brace for disappointment, and filter new experiences through old pain. Slowly, subtly, what could've been an isolated moment of emotion becomes a consistent state of being. That's how a negative emotion becomes a negative mindset.

That's why you must work on your mind like it's sacred ground—daily, deliberately, and with devotion. You have to train your mind so strong that no trigger, no opinion, no storm can break your inner clarity.

And here comes the turning point—why it is absolutely essential to break negative patterns.

Because every time you respond from the same old place—defensiveness, blame, self-doubt—you reinforce a loop that keeps you small. It's like walking the same circle in a maze and wondering why you never find the exit. These patterns don't just shape how you react; they sculpt your identity over time.

They silently write the story you begin to believe about yourself: "I always mess up," "No one understands me," "I'm just not good enough."

But the truth is, you're not broken—you're just repeating. And the beauty of the human mind is that it can be rewired. It can be reconditioned. When you become aware of the triggers that provoke you and choose differently—when you pause, breathe, and respond with clarity—you disrupt the old code. You send a signal to your nervous system that says: We're no longer living from fear. We're leading from strength.

"Your mind can't grow when it's crowded with negativity—it drains your mental energy and blocks progress. Letting go of these patterns frees space for empowering thoughts that inspire true growth."

The N.E.W. Formula: Break the Negative Pattern

- **N** - New Situation, New Response
- **E** - Emotional Awareness Over Emotional Reaction

- **W** - Witness the Trigger, Don't Wear It

N – New Situation, New Response

Most people live on autopilot—repeating the same emotional responses to slightly different situations. But growth begins when we realize that every moment offers a chance to respond differently. "New Situation, New Response" is an invitation to interrupt the old loop. Instead of reacting the way you always have—defending, withdrawing, lashing out—you pause and ask: What would a higher version of me do here?

This isn't about suppressing what you feel—it's about evolving how you express it. A new situation deserves a conscious, considered response, not the recycled emotion from a past wound. When you stop dragging your history into the present, you create space for a better future.

E – Emotional Awareness Over Emotional Reaction

Reactivity is reflex. Awareness is power. The difference between the two is just a breath, but that breath can change everything. When a trigger strikes, most minds instantly react—without thought, without understanding. Emotional awareness means slowing down enough to feel what you're feeling and why. It's about naming the emotion before it names you.

For example, instead of saying, "I'm just angry," ask yourself, "Am I hurt? Am I scared of being misunderstood?" This shift gives you clarity. Emotional awareness turns the volume down on chaos and turns the light on inside the room. You see clearer, respond wiser, and move forward with inner authority.

W – Witness the Trigger, Don't Wear It

A trigger is not an identity—it's just a signal. But many of us take it personally. We wear our emotions like a badge—"I'm anxious," "I'm offended," "I'm rejected"—and it begins to define us. But your power returns the moment you step back and witness what's happening instead of being consumed by it.

This is where emotional mastery lives—not in pretending you don't feel, but in observing your feelings with grace. Say to yourself: "Ah, this is the old story showing up again." You are not the trigger. You are the awareness behind it. And from that place of witnessing, you can choose your next move instead of being ruled by old emotional habits.

TURN EACH NEGATIVE INTO A OPPORTUNITY BREAKING THE NEGATIVE REACTION LOOP

What separates strong minds from fragile ones isn't immunity to failure—it's how they *respond*

to it.

The ones who wish rise, the ones wish to evolve, ***break that* NEGATIVE *pattern***. Here's how you do it:

N – New Situation, Positive Action

Every new moment is an invitation. Instead of repeating the old emotional scripts, choose a better one. One that matches who you're becoming—not who you've been.

E – Evaluate Before You React

Strong minds don't rush to react. They observe. They pause. They ask: *What am I really feeling? What outcome do I want?* That moment of reflection creates power.

G – Ground Yourself in the Present

Negative spirals often live in the past or the imagined future. Breathe. Return to the now. This moment is not your enemy—it's your launchpad.

A – Accept the Emotion, Don't Amplify It

You can feel without fueling. Accepting anger, fear, or disappointment doesn't mean you let them rule you. It means you see them—and still choose better.

T – Turn the Focus Inward

The world will keep triggering you until you learn to master yourself. Look within. Strength comes not from control, but from deep awareness.

I – Initiate a New Thought Loop

Say something empowering: *"I've been here before, and I'm still here."* Interrupt the old story and rewrite a new one—consciously, courageously.

V – Visualize the Strongest You Responding

Picture it: the wiser, more powerful version of you walking through this moment. Not shaken. Not reactive. Calm. Focused. That version is already inside you.

E – Empower Your Next Step

Don't freeze. Do something that moves you forward, even if it's small. Forward motion is the antidote to emotional paralysis.

That's why mastering the mind isn't a one-time act—it's a lifelong devotion. You don't just "fix" your mindset once and expect life to go easy on you. Life *will* test you. Over and over.

Through failure, through loss, through the words that pierce and the moments that shake your core. And in those moments, the strength of your mental training is revealed.

You have to train your mind so fiercely, so repeatedly, that when the storm arrives, you don't collapse into it—you observe it. You witness the chaos, the panic, the rising urge to fall back into the old story. And instead of reacting, you *choose*. You choose to breathe. You choose to

respond with clarity. You choose to not become what you feel. That's where true strength lies— not in avoiding emotional storms, but in standing tall while they rage, untouched at your core.

Remember,

If you don't take charge of your mind, someone else will shape it. If you don't choose your thoughts, the world will choose them for you. And if you don't break the negative patterns, they'll quietly shape a life you never intended to live.

CULTIVATE SELF-COMPASSION

Do you ever find yourself being a little too harsh on... well, yourself? Maybe you didn't handle a situation the way you'd like — and suddenly, your inner critic becomes a full-blown judge, jury, and executioner. Here's the deal: a strong mind doesn't come from constantly being hard on yourself. It comes from social media quote thing. It's a real mental muscle — and like any other strength, it needs training.

Think of self-compassion as mental first aid. You wouldn't tell a friend with a broken leg to "walk it off," right? But somehow, we tell ourselves to "just deal with it" when our thoughts are hurting. The truth?

That approach weakens the mind over time. Strong minds bend; they don't break.

So, how do you start showing up for yourself without turning into your own worst critic? Try this easy little switch:

It's called the *TRU method* — and yes, that's "tru" as in true to yourself.

T – Talk kindly

Notice the way you talk to yourself when things go wrong. Would you say that out loud to your best friend? If not, it's time to change the script. Instead of saying, "I'm such a tired not achieving," try, "Okay, this was tough, but I'm learning." Simple swaps. Big difference.

R – Remind yourself you're human

Sounds obvious, but we forget. Everyone messes up, everyone feels overwhelmed, and everyone doubts themselves. You are not broken — you're just human. That's the most unbreakable truth there is. After all don't forget to love yourself in all different ways.

U – Understand what you need

This part is about listening in. Are you exhausted? Anxious? Hungry? (Yes, even that matters.) Sometimes self-compassion is a warm bath. Sometimes it's boundaries. Sometimes it's just sitting quietly and letting yourself breathe. Strong minds don't ignore their needs — they respect them.

And that's it. TRU. Not a magic pill. Not a self-help chant. Just a simple way to treat yourself like someone you actually care about. Because here's the quiet secret of strong minds — they don't bully themselves into strength. They build it, one gentle step at a time.

How Self-Compassion Builds a Strong Mind

How exactly does being gentler with yourself make your mind stronger? Shouldn't toughness come from pushing harder, raising your standards, and holding yourself to account? That's the common belief. But it's only half the picture. True mental strength isn't about never breaking down. It's about knowing *how to repair* when you do. And self-compassion is your inner repair kit.

1. It builds emotional resilience

Life throws curveballs. Rejection, criticism, failure — they're part of the package. A self-critical mind takes each hit personally and gets stuck in shame. But a self-compassionate mind? It absorbs the impact and keeps moving.

You're not crumbling under the pressure. You're responding. And that's strength.

2. It lowers stress, anxiety, and burnout

When you constantly attack yourself for not doing enough, not being enough, or not getting it all right, your nervous system lives in a constant state of "threat mode." That's what leads to anxiety, perfectionism, and eventual burnout.

Self-compassion signals safety to the brain.

It activates your *parasympathetic nervous system* (the calming one), helping you recover faster and think more clearly.

In other words: when you're kind to yourself, your brain stops fighting you — and starts working with you.

***3. It increases motivation — the healthy kind**

This might surprise you: studies have shown that self-compassionate people are more motivated to improve, not less.

Why? Because when you treat yourself with understanding, you don't fear failure as much. You're not afraid to take risks, try new things, or bounce back if you slip. Instead of saying "I failed, I give up," you say, "I failed, I'll try differently next time."

That's *growth mindset* in action. And it starts with how you talk to yourself when you fail.

***4. It helps you focus and make clearer decisions**

Self-compassion clears out the mental noise of guilt, regret, and overthinking. When your inner voice becomes calmer and more supportive, you can think straighter, plan better, and lead yourself more confidently.

A strong mind isn't busy fighting battles within itself. It's focused, steady, and ready for what comes next.

***5. It makes your relationships healthier**

Let's not forget: the way you treat yourself becomes the blueprint for how you treat others — and how you let them treat you. People with self-compassion are better at setting boundaries, offering genuine support to others, and walking away from toxic dynamics without blaming themselves.

Because when you start respecting yourself, the whole world starts to feel different. Self-compassion doesn't make you soft. It makes you solid.

It helps you stay steady when life is shaky.

It gives you the courage to fail, the grace to forgive, and the strength to begin again — as many times as it takes.

And in the long run? That's what makes a mind unshakable.

"For the one who sees their worth through the world's reflection — understand this: self- compassion is not optional, it's survival. When you don't speak to yourself with strength and truth, your mind becomes an echo chamber of old doubts. And without forgiveness, the past doesn't disappear — it quietly runs your future."

2. BUILDING RESILIENCE FROM WITHIN

- Embrace Discomfort as Growth
- Develop Mental Flexibility
- Practice Mindful Presence
- Reframe Failure as Feedback

EMBRACE DISCOMFORT AS GROWTH

Discomfort is something we often avoid instinctively. From childhood, we are conditioned to move toward ease—toward what is safe, certain, and familiar. But mental strength does not grow in ease. Resilience, by its very nature, is born from stress, challenge, and uncertainty. To work with strong mind, we must learn not to avoid discomfort—but to walk straight into it, with awareness and purpose.

Growth and comfort cannot coexist. Just like muscles need resistance to grow stronger, our minds need pressure to stretch their capacity. The discomfort we feel when facing a hard truth, a painful failure, or a new challenge is not a signal to stop—it's a signal that we are right where we should be.

Psychologists often refer to this as productive discomfort—a temporary period of unease that arises when we challenge our current patterns. It's what happens when we try something new, give up a harmful habit, or face a fear we've long ignored. It feels messy and uncertain—but that's the point. The discomfort is not a sign of failure; it is the evidence of expansion.

Dr. Kelly McGonigal, a health psychologist at Stanford, teaches that stress isn't always harmful—what matters most is how we interpret it. “When you feel discomfort,” she explains, “your body isn’t breaking down—it’s gearing up for resilience.” In other words, what you label as anxiety might actually be energy. What you call awkwardness may be the sound of new neural pathways forming. Reframing the meaning of discomfort is one of the most powerful shifts a strong mind can make.

Most of us have expects that life should be as painless as possible. But this mindset quietly robs us of resilience. If we only ever stay where it’s easy, we never build the internal tools we need to withstand life when it’s not.

In truth, embracing discomfort does not mean seeking pain for its own sake. It means learning to interpret discomfort as data—information that you are engaging with life fully. The key is to lean in with curiosity rather than recoil in fear.

What is this feeling trying to teach me? What strength is being called out of me right now?

Imagine someone who has never lifted weights trying to pick up a heavy barbell. Their muscles tremble. Their grip is unsure. They might even feel like quitting. But what they don’t realize in that moment is that this struggle is exactly the process of strength being built. The shaking isn’t a sign of weakness. It’s a sign of growth.

Similarly, someone navigating emotional discomfort—grief, rejection, failure—might interpret the pain as a flaw or failure. But in truth, those are some of the most fertile grounds for resilience. As author Brené Brown writes, “You can’t get to courage without walking through vulnerability. Period.” That vulnerability—the ache of being stretched, seen, or undone—is not an obstacle to strength. It is the path.

The question is not how to avoid discomfort—but how to work with it, trust it, and eventually even welcome it as a sign that something inside you is waking up.

You might be in a conversation where a criticism hits too close to home. Your instinct is to defend yourself, to shift the blame or explain. But if you resist that pull, even briefly, you create space. That space is where the mind grows stronger. Not because you agreed with the feedback, but because you chose presence over protection.

A strong mind know how to stay present when the feelings come. You can watch them, breathe through them, ask what they're here to reveal. You recognize that the goal is not to feel good all the time—the goal is to feel real, to be honest about what's happening internally, and to not let that discomfort make your decisions for you.

When you adopt this approach, you begin to notice something surprising: the discomfort starts to shift. It becomes more familiar, even useful. You begin to trust yourself in the storm. You begin to learn that survival isn't about escape—it's about capacity. And capacity is built through practice.

In that sense, every small discomfort becomes an invitation. An awkward silence becomes a chance to listen deeper. A moment of doubt becomes a reminder to ground yourself. A difficult decision becomes a mirror for your values. These aren't detours from the path—they are the path

There's a quiet confidence that begins to emerge when you stop fearing discomfort. You no longer need to avoid hard conversations, new challenges, or uncertain outcomes. You've trained your mind to hold steady under pressure—not by pretending things are fine, but by proving, over and over again, that you can stay present without running.

This kind of strength doesn't make you immune to stress or struggle. What it gives you is something more powerful: response over reaction. Instead of flinching, you now breathe. Instead of retreating, you stay.

You begin to realize that your nervous system, just like your muscles, can be trained—and that training begins by choosing to remain conscious when discomfort arises.

Think of someone learning to meditate. In the beginning, their mind constantly wanders. The body itches. The silence feels loud. But over time, by gently bringing their attention back again and again, they build endurance. The discomfort doesn't disappear—but their relationship to it transforms. They no longer see stillness as suffocating, but as empowering.

That same principle applies to emotional resilience. Every time you stay with discomfort instead of numbing it—whether it's sitting with loneliness, riding out anxiety, or allowing sadness to rise—you're practicing. You're learning that emotions are not emergencies. They are waves. And like all waves, they pass.

The moment you stop demanding that life be painless is the moment you begin to access a deeper form of peace. Not the peace of ease, but the peace of capacity. The kind that says: I can hold this. I've held more before. I'm still here.

And each time you hold it again, you grow quietly, steadily, from within.

What makes some people mentally stronger than others is not that they've had fewer challenges. It's that they've learned how to sit in the challenge without turning on themselves. They've built a mind that says, "This hurts, but it's not the end." Instead of collapsing into fear, they lean into self-trust.

This kind of resilience is a daily practice. Not a dramatic overhaul, but quiet repetitions:

*** Choosing to speak honestly, even when your voice shakes.**

*** Staying off autopilot when emotions rise.**

*** Pausing before escaping into comfort.**

*** Letting a situation be uncomfortable, without needing to fix or flee.**

You might not always feel brave in these moments. But you are. Every time you stay when it's hard— every time you face, feel, and move forward—you are rehearsing for life's bigger tests.

Author James Clear writes, "Every action you take is a vote for the type of person you wish to become." If you want to be mentally strong, you must cast votes for resilience—even in the small, ordinary hours. Especially in the small, ordinary hours.

Because strength is not what you show to the world. It's what you choose when no one is watching. It's the quiet discipline of staying with yourself—especially when it would be easier not to.

Let me show you one conversation that might just change the way you think about discomfort forever.

B: I don't know what's wrong with me. Every time things get hard, I just want to quit.

A: That's not weakness. That's your mind trying to protect you from discomfort. It's instinctive. **B:** But isn't that a problem? I want to be stronger—but I feel like I run at the first sign of struggle. **A:** Tell me—have you ever lifted weights?

B: I don't know what's wrong with me. Every time things get hard, I just want to quit.

A: That's not weakness. That's your mind trying to protect you from discomfort. It's instinctive. **B:** But isn't that a problem? I want to be stronger—but I feel like I run at the first sign of struggle. **A:** Let me ask you—did you always know how to swim?

B: No, I was terrified of water at first.

A: What happened when you first got in the pool?

B: I panicked. I flailed. I wanted to get out.

A: Exactly. But did that mean you were incapable of swimming—or just unfamiliar with it?

B: I guess I had to get used to it.

A: And now?

B: Now I can float. I can stay calm.

A: That's what discomfort is like. At first, it feels like drowning. But if you stay with it—if you breathe and don't fight the water—it starts to carry you.

B: So the discomfort isn't the problem... my reaction to it is.

A: Precisely. Growth happens in those moments when you stop thrashing and start trusting. When you feel fear, and choose to stay anyway.

B: It still sounds scary.

A: It is. But not as scary as never learning how to swim. Not as painful as staying on the shore your whole life, wondering what could have been.

B: And the more I practice?

A: The more confident you become. Not because the water changes, but because *you* do.

"Start learning from your discomforts—because one day, you'll look back and realize they were teaching you how to carry your strength.

DEVELOP MENTAL FLEXIBILITY

There's a moment we all face where something unexpected happens—someone says something that catches us off guard, or a plan falls apart—and we freeze. Our minds cling to what should have happened. That's where the tension builds. A rigid mind resists the shift. A flexible one learns to pivot. And that ability to *shift perspective* is the next stage of mental strength.

Mental flexibility doesn't mean you abandon your values or let go of boundaries. It means you can reframe without losing yourself. When a challenge shows up, a rigid mind asks, "Why is this happening to me?" A strong, flexible mind asks, "What can I learn from this?" That one shift changes the entire experience—from something happening to you, to something happening for you.

This kind of thinking takes practice. At first, it feels unnatural. You'll catch yourself going back to the same old patterns—blaming, resisting, shutting down. That's normal. The goal isn't perfection. It's *recovery*. The faster you can catch yourself and shift, the stronger your mind becomes.

And here's something most people miss: being mentally flexible also means being flexible with yourself. Forgiving your past decisions. Letting go of who you thought you had to be. Giving yourself permission to change your mind. Strong minds are not built on constant pressure— they're built on *adjustment*. The ability to bend, soften, redirect, and keep moving forward.

One of the most powerful signs of a strong, flexible mind is the ability to let go of control. That doesn't mean you stop caring or stop trying. It means you stop gripping so tightly that your own expectations become the problem. Life isn't a script. It's more like a dance—messy, improvised, and full of unexpected turns. If you want to move through it with strength, you have to *release the need for certainty*.

People with rigid thinking need everything to be clear, predictable, guaranteed. But flexible thinkers become comfortable in the unknown. They say, "I don't know yet, and that's okay." They understand that not having all the answers isn't a weakness—it's a sign of maturity.

Strength is trusting yourself enough to keep moving, even when the path isn't clear.

This is where growth really happens. When you stop forcing outcomes. When you stop needing everything to make sense right away. When you stop thinking, "This shouldn't be happening," and start asking, "What can I build from this?" That mindset turns chaos into opportunity. It turns discomfort into progress.

And like anything worth having, mental flexibility is something you earn. You build it over time—through the hard conversations you didn't avoid, the changes you learned to accept, and the moments you paused when you wanted to react. Every time you adapt without losing your center, you get stronger.

So no, strength isn't about never bending. It's about knowing when to bend, how to bend, and most importantly—how to bounce back.

That's how strong minds work.

It's easy to believe the first idea that pops into your head is the absolute truth — but often, it's just one perspective among many.

Think about Netflix in the early 2000s. Originally, it was a DVD-by-mail service competing with traditional video rental stores like Blockbuster. When streaming technology started to emerge, Netflix's leadership faced a critical choice: stick to their existing business model or adapt to the new digital age. Instead of clinging to what had worked before, they asked themselves tough questions: Could we imagine a future without physical DVDs? How could we reach customers in a completely different way?

By challenging their own assumptions, Netflix embraced streaming long before it was mainstream. That willingness to rethink their entire approach transformed them from a niche DVD company into a global entertainment powerhouse. If Netflix had resisted change and stuck to the familiar, they would have been outpaced — maybe even disappeared long ago.

This stage isn't about abandoning your ideas but about holding them lightly enough to explore alternatives. When you train yourself to question your thoughts, you unlock new paths and creative solutions that rigid thinking can't see. Flexibility here means curiosity—being willing to ask, "What else is possible?

The final step in developing mental flexibility is the willingness to take action—even when it feels uncomfortable or uncertain. It's one thing to pause and rethink, but quite another to actually change course or try something new. This stage is where many people get stuck, held back by fear or doubt.

Consider Steve Jobs during the development of the iPhone. Early on, Apple was known for its computers and music players. Moving into the smartphone market was risky and uncharted territory. Jobs faced skepticism not only from competitors but also from within his own company. Instead of retreating to what was familiar, he pushed forward with a vision that was bold and different. He embraced trial, error, and change, constantly refining the product until it became the revolutionary device we know today.

This willingness to act in uncertainty, to fail and try again, is the hallmark of mental flexibility in practice. It's about stepping into discomfort, knowing that growth often comes from doing what feels unfamiliar. When you practice this stage, you train your mind to adapt quickly, respond creatively, and keep moving forward despite setbacks.

Developing mental flexibility isn't a one-time event—it's a habit, built through repeated choice and effort. The more you stretch your thinking and behavior, the more natural it becomes to respond to life's challenges with openness and resilience.

These three stages reveal a powerful truth about how our minds grow and adapt. What this shows us is that flexibility is the foundation of a resilient mindset. People who can shift their thinking don't get stuck in a single plan or one way of seeing the world. Instead, they hold multiple options in mind — "If not this, then that" — and prepare themselves to pivot when needed. This mental openness allows them to navigate challenges with creativity rather than frustration.

In essence, mental flexibility is the art of holding firm and letting go at the same time. It's the ability to plan, adapt, and recover — knowing that the path to success is rarely straight. And those who master this balance are equipped not just to survive life's ups and downs, but to turn them into opportunities for growth and achievement.

To understand this profound difference, let's explore the defining characteristics that separate a flexible mind from a non-flexible one. This comparison will illuminate the mindset shifts essential for navigating the complexities of life with resilience and grace.

FLEXIBLE MINDSET		NON-FLEXIBLE
1.Attitude Toward Change.	Sees change as an essential catalyst for growth and innovation; embraces uncertainty with curiosity and optimism	Views change as a disruption to stability; resists new circumstances and clings to familiar comfort zones.
2. Problem-Solving Approach	Approaches challenges with creativity and adaptability, willing to experiment with different solutions until success is found.	Relies on tried-and-true methods; reluctant to alter strategies even when circumstances demand it.
3. Response to Failure	Treats failure as a valuable lesson and stepping stone to improvement, maintaining resilience and motivation.	Interprets failure as a personal defeat, often leading to discouragement and avoidance of future risks.
4. Emotional Regulation	Exercises calm self-awareness, responding thoughtfully rather than	Prone to frustration and emotional outbursts, which impair judgment and escalate tensions.

	reacting impulsively during stress or conflict.	
5. Openness to New Ideas	Actively seeks diverse perspectives and embraces learning opportunities beyond comfort zones.	Prefers familiar viewpoints, often dismissing alternative ideas and limiting intellectual growth.
6. Patience and Persistence	Understands that meaningful progress requires time and steady effort, showing perseverance through setbacks.	Exhibits impatience, seeking quick results and becoming easily discouraged by delays or difficulties.
7. Communication Style	Listens actively and adjusts communication to build rapport and understanding across different personalities.	Holds rigidly to own viewpoints, often resulting in misunderstandings and interpersonal friction
8. Adaptability in Planning	Maintains multiple contingency plans, ready to pivot strategies when obstacles arise or new information emerges.	Sticks stubbornly to original plans, even when evidence suggests the need for change or adjustment.

9. Relationship with Uncertainty	Embraces ambiguity as a fertile ground for innovation, remaining comfortable without all answers upfront.	Experiences anxiety and discomfort in uncertain situations, seeking control to alleviate unease.
10. Gratitude and Perspective	Cultivates gratitude, using it as an anchor to maintain positivity and perspective amid challenges.	Focuses on negatives and setbacks, which perpetuates resistance and narrows the scope for constructive change.

THE POWER OF MINDFUL PRESENCE

Have you ever found yourself in the middle of a conversation, nodding along, yet not truly listening? Or reached the end of a long day only to wonder where it all went—as if you had been there, but not fully? That quiet sense of absence, of drifting through your own life, isn't a defect of character. It's a symptom of a world that moves far too fast for the soul to keep up with.

The antidote is neither complex nor elusive. It is both simple and profound: **the practice of mindful presence**.

Mindful presence is the conscious choice to be fully, unapologetically here. Not entangled in yesterday's regrets. Not racing ahead into tomorrow's demands. But grounded in the one place life truly happens—this moment. It is the gentle art of bringing your awareness back to your breath, your body, your heartbeat, your now.

In a world that glorifies busyness, we often confuse movement with meaning. Productivity is praised as power. But real power is often found not in speed, but in stillness. In the quiet strength that steadies you amid chaos. In the clarity that surfaces when you stop running from discomfort and allow yourself to stay—with presence—long enough to listen to what it's trying to teach you.

You don't have to fix every thought. You don't need to silence every emotion. Mindful presence doesn't demand control—it asks only for your attention. To notice. To observe the swirl of your inner world without needing to control or correct it. Just like watching clouds drift across the sky, you don't chase them. You simply watch. You breathe. You remain.

And in that act of staying, something beautiful unfolds: you remember a truth that has always been there. You are not your thoughts. You are the one who sees them. You are not your fear. You are the one brave enough to feel it. You are not your emotions. You are the space in which they rise and fall.

This gentle shift—a return to presence—is how we begin to live with intention instead of running on autopilot. It is how we cultivate a mind that does more than just endure the storm; it stands steady within it. This is the true essence of mindful presence. It is not a performance. It is not about control. It is about surrender—graceful, conscious surrender to the richness of now.

Imagine yourself in a high-stakes meeting. The atmosphere is charged—ideas fly across the room, voices overlap in a layered hum, and somewhere beneath it all, your mental to-do list buzzes like static. The pressure is palpable. But then something rare occurs. You pause. You breathe. And in that breath, you return.

Amid the noise, a single phrase rises from the clutter. A subtle insight, a buried clue, an opportunity unnoticed by others. This is not coincidence—it is the quiet magic of mindful presence.

Presence is not passive observation. It is active engagement. It sharpens your senses and clears your thinking. It's what allows a student to retrieve a critical fact in the hush of an examination room. It's what steadies the surgeon's hand at the edge of life and death. It's what helps a writer recognize an idea, hold onto it, and shape it into something lasting.

When you are truly present, your mind becomes a fertile ground for insight. You begin to connect the dots others miss. You don't just hear—you *listen.* You don't merely react—you *respond.* Your questions carry weight. Your contributions elevate the entire dialogue. Your instincts grow precise, not because you're trying harder, but because you're *fully here*.

In a fast-moving world, presence is a superpower. It allows you to perceive what's beneath the surface—intentions unspoken, problems unformed, patterns unfolding. It declutters your mind. It anchors your actions in what truly matters.

But the beauty of presence lies not only in its impact on productivity or performance. It is, more deeply, a foundation for personal evolution. It teaches you patience, grows your resilience, and nurtures a calm center that does not waver in the face of uncertainty.

And the more you practice, the more your mind learns to return—to the present, to your breath, to the clarity that lives in stillness. Even in chaos, you begin to find that space within yourself that doesn't flinch or flee, but simply witnesses.

Consider the story of Mary Kom—Olympic boxer, mother, fighter, legend. Picture her in the ring at the 2012 Olympics. The crowd roars. The weight of a nation rests quietly on her shoulders. It's a moment that could easily fracture the mind—most would lose focus under such pressure. But not Mary.

She breathes. She tunes in—not just to the movements of her opponent, but to the rhythm of her own breath, the beat of her heart, the silent wisdom of her body. She does not panic. She does not flinch. She does not react—she *responds.*

That moment of centered stillness became her greatest weapon. It was the edge that turned fear into clarity, tension into timing. The difference between defeat and victory.

But Mary's strength extended beyond the ring. She faced injury. She balanced the demands of motherhood with the discipline of training. She rose in a society not always ready to embrace fierce, ambitious women. Through it all, she returned to the moment—again and again. Her tools? Breath. Awareness. Discipline of the mind. Her real strength wasn't just physical—it was presence.

Mary Kom's journey is a testament to this truth: mastery in any field begins with mastering the mind. And the mind can only be mastered in the present.

Coming Home to Now

So the next time you find yourself in a meeting, a conversation, or a moment of pressure—pause. Breathe. Feel your feet on the floor. Feel the breath in your chest. Come home to now.

Because it is in that stillness—beneath the noise, beneath the mental rush—that something powerful begins to rise. Clarity. Courage. Knowing.

Presence of mind is an invisible superpower. It doesn't announce itself, but it changes everything. It helps you stop reacting blindly and begin shaping your life consciously. It tunes you into the heartbeat of the moment and empowers you to meet it with grace.

So stay with yourself. Not in yesterday's regret. Not in tomorrow's worry. But here. Now. Because *this*—this moment—is where your power live

REFRAME FAILURE AS FEEDBACK

Failure is one of the most universally feared experiences in life Now, this one is not rocket science. If you want to become mentally stronger, more resilient, and grow faster in any area of life, then... you need to stop seeing failure as something negative.

All we need to do is closely examine how people respond to setbacks and mistakes — and then do the opposite of what the average person does. You might not like to think of yourself as someone who fears failure, but truthfully, most of us carry that fear at some level. What sets successful people apart is not that they don't fail — it's that they **see failure as useful data**. This mindset only requires a little practice and a willingness to rethink your perspective.

Think of a person who never seems to take failure personally. What are they like? What do they do differently? You might like to know that a study led by **Carol Dweck** at Stanford University, known for her work on the **growth mindset**, found that people who believe intelligence and ability can develop over time are more likely to embrace failure as part of learning.

None of this should come as a surprise: people who saw mistakes as proof of their incompetence often gave up quickly, while those who treated setbacks as part of the process persisted longer and ultimately succeeded more. In fact, experiments showed that students praised for their effort (rather than their intelligence) were more likely to try again after failing. It's not about avoiding failure — it's about what meaning we assign to it.

Importantly, nowhere in these studies were the participants told they had to like failure—they simply began to interpret it differently. When asked how they felt after a mistake, those with a growth mindset showed more determination, while others showed shame or frustration. The researchers even noted shifts in brain activity: the brain literally **responded more actively** when a person believed they could learn from a mistake.

We should note that this is all about interpretation — failing an exam, missing a promotion, or being rejected is not inherently good or bad. What the research uncovered was that people who **reframed these moments as feedback** rather than judgment were the ones who bounced back faster, grew stronger, and eventually reached higher levels of success.

Something the researchers noted is that this mindset isn't just about academics or career. In relationships, health goals, or even daily habits, reframing failure as feedback helps us adjust, improve, and stay committed. And this brings us to the important point

When dealing with failure, there is always a degree of mental storytelling involved. Truthfully, no failure is meaningless. Every setback contains a lesson, an insight, or a signal pointing us in a better direction. The problem is, we often interpret failure in ways that exaggerate our shortcomings or ignore what the situation is trying to teach us. It's not that we need to sugarcoat our experiences, but we do need to adjust the way we perceive and present them to ourselves.

The mental stereotype of "I failed, so I'm not good enough" actually includes many smaller cognitive missteps — often, a failure is just an event, but we treat it like a label. Some of the most common unhelpful reactions to failure include:

Negative

Self-critical Defensive Rigid Fearful

Overthinking Blaming Quitting Avoidant Hopeless Ashamed Fixed mindset Perfectionistic Excuse-making Passive

Positive

Self-compassionate Curious

Adaptable Brave Reflective Accountable Persistent

Solution-seeking

Optimistic Resilient Growth mindset Realistic Responsible Proactive

These traits fit perfectly with our model of growth as a journey, not a destination. Think about it: why would anyone keep going if failure always felt like a punishment or dead end? When we call an experience a failure and stop there, we are really saying, "This is the end." But the most successful people use failure to redirect, to discover, and to expand. Productive failure is fast, insightful, and leads to evolution. Toxic failure is slow, heavy, and filled with self-blame. The next time you catch yourself spiraling into guilt or regret, remember that this mindset places you firmly in the "stuck" category.

There is one simple method for making sure that you respond to failure in a more empowering way: treat it like feedback. People who grow the fastest are not the ones who never fall — they're the ones who **learn every time they do**. Allow yourself to be a beginner. Welcome

criticism if it's constructive. Focus on setbacks as signals, not stop signs. Be curious. Reflect, reframe, and rise.

You have complete control over how you interpret and talk about your setbacks, and how you present those moments to others — and more importantly, to yourself. If it turns out that you're someone who's used to brushing off failures or hiding them, then you may need to "self-edit" a bit — not to deny what happened, but to look at it through a more constructive lens. Maybe emphasize the growth, the grit, or the lesson learned — not just the fall. That's not being fake. That's being **resilient**.

REMEMBER This

- Reframing failure as feedback is about shifting from judgment to curiosity. First, stop letting your ego define failure as a personal flaw — instead, see it as a natural checkpoint in the process of growth. Failure isn't always about being wrong. It's about finding out what doesn't work — so you can get closer to what does.

- Move steadily through the stages of recovery by first accepting what happened without defensiveness. Reflect openly, without shame. Ask: What can this teach me? What would I do differently next time? This mental shift — from defeat to discovery — is where real resilience is built.

- Use reflection stories when talking about your failures. Instead of hiding them, share them as honest moments that shaped your growth. Talk about the mistake, yes — but also highlight how it changed you, how you adjusted, what strength it revealed in you.

- You come across as emotionally stronger and wiser when you demonstrate that failure doesn't shake your identity — it **sharpens** it. Use phrases like "what I learned from that experience was…" or "that setback actually helped me to…" These statements turn failure into proof of your progress.

- Finally, don't fear failure! Failure is only fatal if you refuse to learn from it. In life, be curious, brave, honest, and flexible — and don't cling to the need to always succeed on the first try. Growth doesn't require perfection. It requires **perspective**.

3. MASTERING YOUR INNER DIALOGUE

- Challenge Limiting Beliefs
- Speak to Yourself Like a Leader
- Harness the Power of Affirmations
- Silence the Inner Critic

CHALLENGE LIMITING BELIEFS

Almost everyone has heard about the power of positive thinking and how mindset shapes our reality, but relatively few of us stop to question the actual thoughts running through our minds every day. However, your inner dialogue is not just background noise — it is a stream of beliefs, assumptions, and silent rules that shape every decision you make. When you think about it, your thoughts are the script your life quietly follows.

The beliefs you carry matter, but the ones you never question may matter even more. Limiting beliefs often disguise themselves as facts. They can sound like, "I'm not good enough," "That's just how I am," or "It's too late for me." These statements often go unchallenged because they've lived in your mind for so long, they feel familiar — but familiarity doesn't make something true. A single limiting belief can keep you from pursuing an opportunity, deepening a relationship, or stepping into your potential.

The thing to remember about limiting beliefs is that they are not truths — they are emotional impressions, and because of that, they are often accepted before they are even examined.

Rather than thinking of your limiting beliefs as fixed truths, understand that they are often emotional filters shaping how you interpret your experiences. These beliefs aren't just cold, hard facts—they carry emotional weight that influences your decisions and reactions, sometimes without you even realizing it.

Psychologist Carol Dweck's groundbreaking research showed that individuals with a fixed mindset—who believe their abilities and intelligence are static—often avoid challenges and give up easily. They may know logically that trying can help them grow, but emotionally, the fear of failure and judgment holds them back. Without addressing the feelings tied to these beliefs, changing them is almost impossible.

So, how do you begin to challenge these limiting beliefs? The approach depends on your awareness, willingness to reflect, and the context of your inner dialogue. Start by identifying beliefs that hold you back, then gently question their validity. Ask yourself: Where did this belief come from? Is it always true? What evidence do I have to the contrary?

Consider these practical elements in your inner dialogue:

- Awareness
- Inquiry
- Compassionate curiosity
- Gradual transformation

Each element helps you untangle the emotional grip of limiting beliefs and gradually replace them with empowering alternatives.

Be mindful of how you engage with your limiting beliefs in different situations. Sometimes, being too harsh or critical with yourself can reinforce low self-esteem and self-doubt. On the other hand, approaching these beliefs gently—acknowledging their presence without judgment— can create space for real change. When you notice a limiting belief creeping in, pause and bring your full attention to it, like drawing closer to a whisper that needs to be heard and understood.

The intensity with which you challenge a belief matters. Push too hard, and you might trigger defensiveness or anxiety. Challenge too softly, and the belief may stay rooted, unexamined. Finding the right balance is key—enough pressure to question the belief, but enough compassion to keep you engaged and curious.

Pace yourself through this process. Rapid self-criticism or trying to overhaul your mindset overnight often leads to overwhelm and discouragement. Moving too slowly, however, can mean staying stuck in old patterns longer than necessary. Gradually, with steady practice, you'll build confidence in recognizing and reshaping your inner narrative.

One practical way to challenge limiting beliefs is to bring them out into the open and examine them closely. Write down a belief you hold about yourself—perhaps something like "I'm not good enough" or "I always fail." Then, question it as if you were a curious investigator. Where did this belief start? What evidence supports it? What evidence contradicts it? This kind of reflective practice is like rehearsing a speech—you get to observe your thoughts and learn how they affect your emotions and actions.

Your inner dialogue shapes your self-image and confidence. If you constantly tell yourself you can't succeed, your behavior will align with that story. To shift this, practice affirming your strengths and possibilities, even if it feels awkward at first. This isn't about blind positivity, but about nurturing a realistic and kinder narrative that supports growth. When you notice your mind racing with doubts, take a moment to pause and breathe. Ask yourself if those doubts truly serve you, or if they're just limiting beliefs holding you back.

If you find your limiting beliefs deeply rooted, consider seeking perspectives from trusted friends, mentors, or professionals who can offer an outside view. Sometimes we are blind to our own patterns, and having a mirror held up by others can reveal hidden stories that no longer serve us. The key question is: Are your beliefs empowering you to be your best self, or are they barriers to your growth? If it's the latter, it's time to gently but firmly challenge and reframe them.

"Sometimes, we repeat a thought so many times, it turns into a belief — and we forget it was once just an option, not a fact.\

SPEAK TO YOURSELF LIKE A LEADER

Imagine your inner dialogue as a captain guiding a ship through unknown waters. If that voice speaks with panic, confusion, or criticism, the crew will lose confidence, and the ship will drift aimlessly. But if the voice is steady, calm, and commanding, the crew holds steady—even through the storm. Leaders speak to their teams with conviction. You must speak to yourself the same way.

Think of your self-talk as the internal blueprint that builds your outer reality

There's a well-known psychological principle: cognitive framing. The way you talk to yourself literally changes the way you perceive a situation. If you call a setback a disaster, you act like it's unfixable. But if you reframe it as a lesson, your brain starts searching for solutions. A true leader doesn't just face the facts—they shape the narrative around those facts in a way that fuels action, not fear.

You wouldn't follow a leader who constantly second-guessed their every move or belittled their team. So why tolerate that voice inside your own head? Leading yourself means using inner language that's firm yet fair, courageous yet honest. It means replacing blame with responsibility, criticism with strategy, and fear with curiosity. It's about speaking to yourself the way a mentor would—someone who believes in your potential even when you stumble.

You don't have to shout affirmations or pretend everything is perfect. You simply need to shift from self-judgment to self-command. Instead of saying, "I can't handle this," try, "Let's take it one step at a time." Instead of "I always mess up," say, "This is where I grow." That shift in tone changes everything—from your emotions to your actions.

So the next time your inner critic shows up, pause. Ask yourself: Would a strong, grounded leader speak like this? If not, rewrite the script. Because the most powerful leadership starts not with how you speak to others, but how you speak to yourself.Because we have countless associations with the concept of leadership—strength, clarity, vision—we respond differently when we adopt this tone internally. Speaking to yourself like a leader activates those associations. Your words carry more weight, your thoughts sound more purposeful, and your actions begin to follow. The language of leadership isn't about pretending to be perfect. It's about communicating with your inner self in a way that uplifts, directs, and empowers.

The same thing happens when we reshape our self-talk from vague negativity to clear, powerful metaphors of growth. When you say, "I'm climbing a mountain," your mind prepares for effort and progress. When you say, "I'm drowning," your body reacts with fear and defeat. The metaphor matters. It paints your inner world. Leaders know this—so they choose the imagery of hope, strategy, and movement.

The human brain thrives on meaningful internal narratives. It remembers stories better than facts and grows stronger through emotionally charged associations. When you speak to yourself with the richness of a leader—using metaphors, vision, and a sense of direction—you engage your entire mind in the process of becoming stronger. You become your own motivational speaker, coach, and guide.

Think of the leaders who've inspired you. They likely spoke in a way that helped you see your own potential more clearly. They didn't just give you steps—they gave you belief. When you mirror that same clarity and authority in your own thoughts, you do something powerful: you create a relationship with yourself based on trust and leadership.

Charisma, as it turns out, is not reserved for public figures. It can show up in your mirror when you speak to yourself with certainty, empathy, and purpose. Internal charisma makes you magnetic not just to others, but to your own goals. Vivid self-talk lights the path when motivation fades, and reminds you why you began in the first place.

One of the greatest strengths of speaking to yourself like a leader is that you don't have to over- explain, justify, or overthink. A few strong, steady words can shift your mood, your posture, even your day. You can go from "I can't do this" to "I lead myself through this" with just a change in tone—and that difference is enough to move mountains.

So, what do you care most about? What kind of leader do you want to follow? Then become that leader—for yourself. Craft the metaphors, choose the tone, and direct your inner dialogue like the mind of someone who has already claimed their strength.

For example, you could imagine talking to yourself like a wise mentor, saying, "Facing challenges is like climbing a steep mountain with a trusted map in hand, even when the weather is uncertain."

Whenever you craft an analogy like this internally, you're helping your mind digest complex emotions and thoughts more easily. Metaphors like these don't just pass along ideas—they show you how to feel about those ideas and how they fit into the bigger picture of your life. They give meaning and direction.

Leaders have mastered this kind of self-talk to inspire themselves, stay motivated, and stay grounded. But you can use this approach to deepen your self-awareness, increase your resilience, and cultivate a stronger, more supportive internal conversation.

To borrow from the wisdom of great leaders, here are some tips for speaking to yourself with vivid, impactful language:

Don't just repeat what you think you should do or feel. Try to understand what your inner self really needs to hear, and frame your thoughts in a way that resonates deeply. Speak to yourself as if you truly understand yourself—and as if your inner voice deserves respect and encouragement

Don't let your inner voice become dull or repetitive. Even in the smallest moments, keep your self-talk vibrant and engaging. People who think with vivid and compelling language experience greater clarity and confidence. So, avoid bland, worn-out phrases inside your mind—be creative with your words. Use strong, unusual adjectives or inspiring images that make your inner dialogue stand out and feel meaningful.

Let your genuine passion for your own growth shine through your thoughts. When you reflect on your progress or challenges, connect with the emotional heart of the experience. Speak to yourself with warmth, encouragement, and belief, as if cheering from the sidelines with unwavering support.

Resist the urge to recycle the same tired messages over and over. One powerful, clear thought that truly resonates with you is far more effective than many weak or half-hearted ones. Give yourself the gift of focused, meaningful inner speech that moves you forward.

"Leadership begins in the mind—when you choose to believe in your own potential, you unlock the power to shape your reality and inspire others to follow."

Lastly, Be Great.

Be Leader. Be Your Best.

No matter what is in your own mind, but be the leader every time.

HARNESS THE POWER OF AFFIRMATIONS

As the name suggests, affirmations are positive statements you tell yourself deliberately to influence your mindset and beliefs. You might already be familiar with simple affirmations like "I am confident" or "I can do this," but harnessing their true power goes far beyond just repeating nice phrases.

For example: "Every morning, I stand in front of the mirror and say, 'I am becoming stronger every day.' At first, it felt strange—like I was just saying words—but over time, those words started to feel like a reality I was creating."

This example shows how affirmations begin as simple sentences but gradually build into a deep, internal conviction. Why is this important? The key benefit of affirmations is that they rewire your subconscious mind, replacing limiting beliefs with empowering ones—helping you steer your thoughts and actions in a positive direction

People who master affirmations often use them like seeds planted in the mind—simple phrases they return to again and again, letting those words grow stronger over time. Just like comedians leaving open loops for punchlines later, affirmations are not just one-off statements. They're reminders you come back to, reinforcing your belief in yourself bit by bit.

Naturally confident people don't just say affirmations once and forget them. They repeat them with feeling and conviction, sometimes mixing them into daily routines so they become second nature. Have you ever noticed how some people seem calm and centered no matter what? Much of that comes from a steady habit of positive self-talk that keeps their mindset anchored.

You don't have to force yourself to declare a long list of affirmations every day. Instead, start small and be consistent. Keep your affirmations flexible and meaningful, allowing them to evolve with you. By holding back a little—avoiding overloading yourself with too many statements—you leave room for growth and deeper belief to build naturally over time.

You don't need to craft perfect affirmations that end all doubt instantly. Instead, let them be open-ended prompts that you revisit often. This keeps your inner dialogue fresh and adaptable, inviting ongoing change and renewed confidence.

Affirmations are like a conversation you have with yourself—there's no need to over-explain or tie everything up neatly. In fact, the most powerful affirmations are often the ones you leave open-ended, allowing them to grow and shift as your experiences change. They become a source of steady encouragement, ready to support you exactly when you need it most.

This power comes from how affirmations interact with your subconscious mind. Unlike your conscious mind, the subconscious doesn't distinguish between what's real and what's imagined. It simply accepts repeated statements as truth and adjusts your beliefs, feelings, and actions accordingly.

HERE ARE SOME SECRETS TO HARNESS THE POWER OF AFFIRMATIONS,

Secret 1: Your Words Create Your Reality

Understand this clearly: your mind does not distinguish between what you say and what you believe. Repeating positive affirmations isn't mere repetition—it's a deliberate rewiring of your brain's core beliefs. Speak your truth often enough, and your mind will start living it as reality.

Secret 2: Emotion is the Catalyst That Brings Affirmations to Life

Affirmations are far more than words—they are feelings given voice. When you declare, *"I am confident,"* don't just say it; feel that confidence surge through your body. Emotion is the spark that ignites lasting transformation.

Secret 3: Consistency Outweighs Intensity

You don't need hours of affirmations every day. The true power lies in habit—committing to a daily practice, whether morning, afternoon, or night. Small, consistent steps build an unshakable mental foundation.

Secret 4: Always Speak in the Present Tense

Frame your affirmations as if they are happening now. Say *"I am strong"* instead of *"I will be strong."* Your mind is wired to act on what is immediate. The present tense compels your brain to embody the change today.

Secret 5: Make Your Affirmations Personal and Relevant

One-size-fits-all affirmations fall flat. The ones that resonate deepest are tailored to your values, goals, and aspirations. Craft affirmations that reflect your unique path—this makes them unforgettable and effective.

Secret 6: Use Affirmations to Silence Negative Self-Talk

Catch your mind when it drifts into doubt or defeat. Immediately counter those thoughts with affirmations of strength and possibility. If the thought says, *"I can't,"* respond firmly, *"I am capable and unstoppable."* This conscious pushback reshapes your inner narrative.

Secret 7: Pair Affirmations with Vivid Visualization

See yourself living your affirmations fully. Picture yourself calm, courageous, or focused—the qualities you want to cultivate. Visualization acts like a mental rehearsal, reinforcing the message until it becomes second nature.

Secret 8: Treat Affirmations as Your Personal Inner Coach

Think of your affirmations as your own internal cheerleader, offering unwavering encouragement even when external circumstances challenge you. They are your steady source of motivation and resilience.

Secret 9: Lean on Affirmations Before, During, and After Challenges

Whether preparing for a big moment, navigating stress, or recovering from setbacks, affirmations steady your mind. They keep your inner dialogue constructive and your focus sharp, no matter the obstacle.

Secret 10: Believe in the Power of Your Voice Above All

The ultimate secret is this: your words hold the power to transform your mind—and by extension, your life. Your inner voice can be your greatest ally or your harshest critic. Choose to make it your most powerful source of strength.

"These secrets are the keys to mastering your inner dialogue and forging a resilient, focused mind."

SILENCE INNER CRITICS

Here's a tough truth that many people avoid—but acknowledging it is the first step toward mental freedom: the harsh voice in your head isn't helping you grow.

The mind has a tendency to replay old criticisms, internalize others' judgments, and turn them into a constant loop of criticism. Over time, you may start believing these thoughts are who you really are. But here's the fact: your inner critic is not your identity. It's just a thought pattern— and like any pattern, it can be changed.

Think of your inner critic like a bad roommate. They talk nonstop, criticize your every move, and yet contribute nothing helpful. Would you let someone like that live in your house rent-free? No. Then why allow them to occupy your mental space without challenge? Silencing the inner critic doesn't mean pretending problems don't exist—it means refusing to allow fear-based thinking to steer your life.

So how do you quiet this voice? You start by recognizing when it shows up. Pay attention to the language: is it judgmental, harsh, or discouraging? Does it focus on failure or fear? Once you notice it, pause. Don't argue or fight it—simply step back. The power comes from creating distance between *you* and the thought. Over time, as you speak to yourself with more care, the voice of the inner critic grows quieter, and the voice of your inner coach gets louder.

Now, you don't need to become hyper-aware and second-guess every thought that crosses your mind. Silencing the inner critic doesn't mean you mute your brain entirely—it means you begin to understand its patterns and take back control. Just like you can train yourself to speak within a minute in conversations, you can also train your thoughts to follow a healthier, more helpful rhythm

Your brain will often default to negativity not because it's true, but because it's familiar. That's not a flaw—it's conditioning. But if you want a strong mind, you have to condition it differently. Learn to notice when the voice in your head is just repeating an old script and not reflecting the current truth of who you are.

And here's the key—don't argue with the inner critic. That only gives it more power. Instead, give it less airtime. "Keep them brief, like the punchlines of a good story.

And if you're wondering—what if the inner critic keeps talking even when you've learned to notice it? Here's your answer: you don't have to entertain every thought that shows up. Just because your mind throws a thought doesn't mean you have to catch it. You can let it pass, just like you can let a rambler finish speaking without engaging.

Sometimes, we cling to our inner critic because we fear that letting go will make us careless or too soft on ourselves. But self-compassion isn't laziness. It's resilience in disguise. Giving your inner encourager more space to speak doesn't make you arrogant—it makes you human.

Think of your mental dialogue like a conversation with a friend. If one person dominates the entire exchange, it becomes exhausting. A healthy inner world requires balance. You must learn when to hold the space for understanding and when to challenge harmful thoughts with strength and grace. It's not a tug of war with your mind. It's a tennis match—bounce the ball, and let the dialogue stay alive and kind.

A great trick is this: when you hear that harsh voice judging you, don't fight it—pivot. Say something like, "That's not the full story," or "There's more to me than that." You shift the direction. You take back control. Slowly, you'll train your mind to recognize criticism without making it the main character of your inner narrative.

And yes—sometimes your inner critic will still press for attention. It will remind you of old fears, past mistakes, and all the things you should've done better. But here's your power: you don't have to finish the story it begins. You can leave space, pause, or even say, "That's enough for now." Strength isn't about shouting louder. It's about choosing which voice deserves your energy.

Think of your inner dialogue like a mental environment. The critic pollutes it. Encouraging self-talk clears the air. When you nurture this space—by journaling, using affirmations, or simply pausing before reacting—you create a mind that supports you instead of sabotaging you. The goal isn't to eliminate the critic completely. The goal is to make sure it's not the one leading your life

There once was a woman named Rama. She wasn't the loudest person in the room, nor did she seem destined for great success. Growing up in a small town, Rama often felt the weight of doubt—both from the people around her and, most challengingly, from within herself.

Everywhere she turned, voices whispered that she wasn't good enough. "You're not ready," they said. "Why even try?" The harshest voice of all, however, was her own inner critic, constantly questioning her worth and abilities. Some days, the self-doubt was so loud, Rama almost believed it.

But instead of surrendering, Rama made a conscious choice: she would stop feeding the critic's voice and start nurturing a different kind of conversation—one rooted in encouragement and belief. Each morning, she repeated quiet affirmations: *I am capable. I am worthy. I can grow.*

This simple daily practice rewired her mindset. Slowly but surely, Rama began to trust herself more. When setbacks came—and they always do—she no longer saw them as failures but as lessons to learn from. The noise of external critics faded, unable to compete with the strength of her newfound inner voice.

Years later, Rama's journey took her to a place she had only once dreamed of—a thriving career and a life built on confidence and resilience. When people asked her how she did it, Rama's answer was always the same:

"The secret isn't in silencing the critics by shouting louder. It's in mastering the dialogue within. When your inner voice is strong, calm, and kind, the outside noise loses its power."

Rama's story is not unique, but it is powerful. It shows us that the greatest battles are often fought quietly, inside our own minds. And winning those battles means learning to silence the inner critic—not by fighting harder, but by listening differently.

SO, Silent DoubtS, Loud StrengthS.

Rise Above, Believe Always

4. TAKING CONTROL OF YOUR REACTIONS

- Pause Before You Respond
- Shift From Impulse to Intention
- Use Breath and Grounding Techniques
- Manage Stress Without Avoidance

PAUSE BEFORE YOU RESPOND

Sometimes, the strongest response is the one you choose *not* to give right away. In conversations—and in life—our natural instinct is often a rapid, knee-jerk reaction: loud, impulsive, and fueled by emotion. But true strength does not lie in how quickly you speak; it lies in the wisdom of how deliberately you respond.

A pause before you answer is like a breath between two crashing waves. It creates a vital space—space for clarity, for sorting through your emotions, for grounding yourself. This moment of stillness is power. It allows you to avoid words that might wound or regret, and instead to speak with purpose and intention. Just as silence deepens a conversation, pausing before you respond deepens your understanding and control.

The pause is your greatest ally. It transforms reaction into choice, chaos into calm, and wild impulses into steady direction.

A positive mind know the value of this pause—not just in speech, but in every moment of emotional intensity. Imagine how differently conversations would unfold if you allowed yourself that brief moment before replying. That pause at difficult moments will be a sanctuary for thought and calm. This pause does more than prevent mistakes—it opens the door to self- reflection. You begin to notice the subtle emotions beneath the surface of your first impulse. Are you hurt, defensive, surprised? Recognizing these feelings lets you respond not from reflex, but with conscious choice.

Moreover, pausing before you speak sends a powerful message to others: it shows them that you listen, that you respect the moment—and them. Your calm presence shifts the energy from conflict to understanding, inviting connection rather than division.

When you make pausing a habit, you radiate calm confidence and quiet authority—a presence others can't help but respect.

Reflect for a moment—have you ever regretted speaking too carelessly?

Almost never. Yet, how often have you found yourself regretting a rushed reply, a hasty reaction, or words spoken without thoughtful clarity? A pause before you respond gifts you precious time to center yourself, question your motives, and ensure your response truly fits the moment. More than that, a thoughtful pause opens space—not just for you to gather your thoughts, but for your listeners to absorb what has been said.

It becomes especially important when the question posed is difficult, when crafting the right answer requires careful thought, or when you need to fully understand what is being asked before responding. Taking that moment to pause allows your mind to process the challenge clearly, gather your thoughts, and choose your words with precision. It helps you navigate complexity with calm and confidence, ensuring your response is thoughtful. In this way, the power of the pause guides you to respond not just quickly—but wisely.

Taking a deliberate pause before responding is one of the simplest yet most profound ways to strengthen your mind. In those brief moments of silence, your brain transitions from reactive impulses to thoughtful reflection. By cultivating this habit, you train your mind to slow down, engage more deeply, and respond properly.

This practice not only sharpens decision-making and reduces misunderstandings but also lessens the chances of regret. Ultimately, it builds mental resilience, sharpens your intellect, and nurtures the calm, focused presence that defines strong minds.

During a widely followed podcast, the host posed a challenging question to Maya—a question layered with complexity, one that demanded more than a quick, off-the-cuff response. The microphone was live, thousands were listening, and a hush fell over the room. Instead of rushing to fill the silence, Maya chose to embrace it. She took a deep, steadying breath, allowing herself the precious seconds to fully grasp the question, gather her thoughts, and frame an answer that was both clear and insightful.

When Maya finally spoke, her words resonated with calm confidence. The audience was captivated—not just by what she said, but by the presence she carried in that moment. That brief pause, invisible to listeners, transformed a potentially stressful moment into one of undeniable strength and clarity. Because, in truth, people don't remember the silence—they remember the wisdom and composure behind the words.

This story beautifully illustrates why pausing before responding is a powerful tool. When faced with difficult questions, complex conversations, or emotionally charged situations, that intentional pause shifts your mind from reactive impulse to thoughtful action. It elevates your communication, strengthens your presence, and showcases the hallmark of strong minds.

Remember: the pause is your hidden strength. Though silent and unseen, it anchors your ability to respond with intention, resilience, and grace. Pause—not merely to catch your breath, but to take control of your reactions and reveal the true power of your mind.

SHIFT FROM IMPULSE TO INTENTION

There is a hidden war that happens within us—every single day. It's not loud or violent. It doesn't make headlines. But it shapes the quality of our lives more than almost anything else.

It's the war between impulse and intention.

Impulse is raw. It bursts out without permission. It wants immediacy, dominance, and relief. It's the raised voice in an argument, the regrettable message sent in anger, the split-second yes when a no was wiser. Impulse rarely asks questions. It assumes. It acts. It escapes discomfort by leaping into action—too fast, too often.

But intention? Intention is mature. It waits in the shadows, observing. It lets the storm pass before deciding how to step forward. It holds back when the ego wants to rush in. Intention isn't slower because it's weak—it's slower because it's wise.

Why do we so often fall into impulsive behavior? Because the brain is wired for survival, not grace. Because reacting feels safer than sitting in uncertainty. Because we confuse speed with strength.

But strong minds don't confuse movement with progress.

They know that real strength lies in restraint. In that silent space between stimulus and response. That pause—tiny as it may be—is where mastery lives.

When we train ourselves to shift from impulse to intention, we reclaim power over the only thing we truly own: ourselves. We stop handing over our emotions to the chaos around us. We begin to shape our responses with clarity, not fear. With vision, and not habit.

It's not always easy. Sometimes, the impulse is loud and convincing. But every time you choose to pause—every time you resist the urge to blurt, snap, or defend—you build a quieter, deeper kind of strength.

Some habits aren't loud at first. They quietly take root in childhood and grow unnoticed into adulthood. One such habit—rushing to speak—often develops in homes where voices clashed for attention. In families where being heard was a fight, children learned to speak quickly, to over- explain, to keep talking just long enough to not be interrupted.

But the roots of this behavior often go deeper than childhood noise. Sometimes, even in silence, people feel the urge to perform. Beneath that urge is often something more fragile: low self- worth disguised as confidence.

Self-doubt doesn't always look like shyness. At times, it shows up in fast speech, nervous talking, and a deep discomfort with silence. The inner dialogue isn't "I am worth listening to," but rather, "I need to prove I'm interesting or I'll lose their attention."

The way to shift from this anxious performance to calm presence is simple but powerful: stop treating every conversation like a test or a stage. You are not being evaluated. You don't need to entertain, persuade, or fill every gap with noise.

Instead, trust that what you say—when said with intention—has weight. Take your time. Savor each word before moving to the next. You are not in a hurry to prove anything..

Where should you pause? Let it be natural. Pause the way a writer uses punctuation: a breath at the comma, a moment of silence after a strong point. Pause before you say something meaningful. Pause when asking a rhetorical question. Let your stillness speak as much as your words.

When you learn to shift from impulse to intention, from rushing to presence, you don't just sound better—you feel better. And more importantly, you begin to live from a deeper place of strength.

Most people don't realize how often they are reacting, not responding. In conversations, in conflict, in pressure—they act out of habit, emotion, and urgency. But strong minds are not pulled by impulse. They are anchored by intention.

Think about it: how often have you rushed to explain, to justify, to fill silence with words—only to regret it afterward? This isn't just about overtalking. It's about the deeper anxiety of being misunderstood, ignored, or unseen.

And it often stems from something deeper than the surface moment.

People who were constantly interrupted, overlooked, or criticized growing up often develop a reflex to over-speak. They race through sentences. They try to prove their worth with speed. Beneath that, there's often a belief: *If I don't get it all out now, I won't get another chance.*

But intention begins where fear ends.

To shift from impulse to intention, you must first make peace with silence. You must learn to breathe before you speak. You must begin to value depth over speed. You're not racing against anyone. You're not in a competition to be the loudest, smartest, or fastest voice in the room.

You're just showing up—with presence.

When you take your time, something powerful happens. Your energy becomes calmer. Your words feel stronger. You're no longer trying to perform. You're grounded in your truth.

And here's the secret: the world listens more when you speak less, but with purpose.

So pause—not because you're unsure, but because you're deliberate. Let silence become part of your strength. Speak only what matters, and you'll find your voice carries more weight.

That is how strong minds communicate. Not in the rush, but in the rhythm of calm confidence.

USE BREATH AND GROUNDING TECHNIQUES

There's a moment—before you speak, before you react, before you move—where choice exists. And in that sliver of time, your breath is waiting.

The breath is the gateway between the body and the mind. It is the most powerful tool you have for turning unconscious reactions into intentional responses. Yet most people overlook it entirely.

Instead, they react. They tighten up. Their breath becomes shallow, fast, almost invisible. In that state, the nervous system shifts into survival mode—what we call "fight or flight." It's not just physical. It affects how you think, how you speak, and how clearly you can access your intelligence.

To build a strong mind, understand this truth: when your breath is erratic, your mind becomes restless. But the moment you breathe with awareness, you reclaim your inner command."**Breathe to Stabilize Your Mind**

Grounding: From Reaction to Presence

Alongside the breath, grounding is your second ally.

To ground yourself means to reconnect with the present moment—physically, mentally, emotionally. When you're grounded, you're not being pulled into the chaos of your thoughts. You're here. Rooted. Aware.

Grounding can be as simple as pressing your feet firmly into the floor. Noticing the texture of your seat. Feeling the air against your skin. When you ground your awareness in the body, your mind begins to slow down.

You stop rushing. You stop trying to prove. You just *are*.

One of the most powerful practices is this: before you speak, feel the ground beneath you. Let your breath settle. Let the body find stillness. Then, speak from that place. Not from tension. Not from defense. From clarity.

You can hear the difference.

A voice that's rushed, tight, and uncertain sounds anxious—even if the words are intelligent. But a voice that's grounded, paced, and intentional—now that voice carries weight. It slows the room down. It earns trust. Not by force, but by presence.

The goal is not perfection. It's awareness.

And the more you practice using the breath to ground yourself—before hard conversations, during moments of overwhelm, at the edge of anger—the more you strengthen your mind. You start to act from wisdom, not impulse.

That's when you'll notice the shift: people listen more. You interrupt less. You feel lighter. Clearer. Aligned.

Before we dive into the techniques, there's something important I want you to know. What I'm about to share isn't based on fluff or quick fixes. These are proven, practical methods that have stood the test of time. You might forget other advice along the way, but once you start practicing these, they'll become part of your routine—because they truly work. And every time you use them, you'll feel the difference.

1. **Tongue-Shift Reset**

One of the simplest yet most effective ways to calm your mind and body begins with your tongue. By slowly moving your tongue from left to right inside your mouth, you stimulate facial nerves that connect directly to your parasympathetic nervous system—the part of your body responsible for relaxation and rest.

Benefit- This calms your brain and lowers physical tension—especially in the jaw and neck, where stress collects silently.

2. **Exhale With a Hum**

When you take a deep breath in and release it slowly while humming softly, you awaken the vagus nerve, the body's natural pacemaker for relaxation. This humming lengthens your exhale, inviting calm into your nervous system.

Benefit: Stimulates the vagus nerve and lengthens the exhale. This helps reduce anxiety, steady the heart rate, and soothe overactive thoughts almost immediately.

Thumb-to-Finger Tapping

In the gentle rhythm of tapping your thumb to each fingertip—index, middle, ring, and pinky— you create a small but powerful bridge between body and mind.Each tap sends subtle signals through your nervous system, encouraging calm and focus while quieting the mind's usual chatter.

Benefit: Brings your focus to the present and helps interrupt overthinking. Used in cognitive- behavioral grounding, it's especially helpful during emotional overwhelm.

3. Pursed-Lip Breathing

Inhale normally, exhale slowly through pursed lips as if blowing through a straw. . With each measured exhale, your nervous system receives a clear message: it's time to relax.

Benefit: Reduces rapid heart rate and supports oxygen-carbon dioxide balance. Used in medical settings to manage anxiety and breathlessness

4. **Wiggle Your Toes**

Gently moving your toes inside your shoes or pressing them into the ground helps you reconnect with your body and the present moment. This simple action awakens nerves, reduces stress,

Benefit: Reconnects your brain to the lower body, pulling awareness down from racing thoughts. Grounding your feet can reduce the feeling of panic or being "stuck in your head." and brings a quick sense of calm and stability

5. Say "Release" as You Exhale

Whisper or think the word "release…" as you breathe out.As you breathe out, gently whisper or mentally repeat the word "release." \

Benefit: Combining intention with breath cues your body to let go—mentally and physically. This encourages emotional processing instead of holding tension.

6. **Slow Blinking**

Blink slowly and intentionally three times.

Benefit- This simple act relaxes the eye muscles, calms the nervous system, and helps reset mental focus.

7. **Rub Palms Together, Then Rest on Heart**

Warm your hands by rubbing, then place them over your chest.

Benefit: Physical warmth and self-touch trigger oxytocin, the calming hormone. This creates a sense of safety and reduces loneliness or emotional tension.

"You don't need hours of meditation to feel better. Sometimes, just one moment of awareness, paired with a small action, is enough to shift your energy and center your mind. The more you use these techniques, the more your body learns what calm feels like—and how to return to it"

MANAGE STRESS WITHOUT AVOIDANCE

Stress is common. Stress is natural. Everyone feels it.

We often mistake avoidance for control. We think: *If I ignore this pressure, it might go away.* But stress is not a stray animal—it doesn't leave when you stop looking. It lingers. It tightens. And the more you try to outrun it, the more it weaves itself into your breath, your posture, your voice.

Stress, in its raw form, is not the enemy. It's a messenger. It tells you that something matters. That something is misaligned. That somewhere, you are carrying more than you need to, or perhaps holding back more than you should. But here's what most people miss: You cannot heal what you won't feel.

But here's the part we don't talk about enough: **just because stress is normal doesn't mean we should let it become our "new normal."**

You're not meant to wake up already exhausted. You're not meant to go through the day with a tight chest and a scattered mind. That's not life. That's survival on autopilot.

We often say, "I'm just stressed" and brush it off — as if it's a small thing. But the truth is, stress that lingers affects everything: the way you talk to the people you love, the way you eat, sleep, even breathe. It affects how you make decisions. It steals your joy and patience, inch by inch.

So why avoid stress? Because your mind needs space to breathe. Your body needs rest to repair. Your relationships need presence and patience. And your spirit? It needs stillness to stay alive.

Avoiding stress doesn't mean avoiding responsibility. It means *managing pressure before it takes over your personality.* It means knowing your limits and listening to your body before it screams for help.

It's not weakness. ***It's wisdom. It's self-respect.***

The world may not slow down. But **you can learn to slow down inside yourself**. You can learn when to pause. When to breathe. When to walk away from what drains you, and walk toward what restores you.

Because yes, stress is real — but so is your power to handle it differently. Stress unmanaged becomes tension. But stress understood becomes direction.

Before you read further, let me tell you something simple — something most people overlook because it sounds too boring to be powerful. But it works. If you ever find yourself caught in the grip of stress, where your mind feels foggy and everything around you feels like too much, **move your body**. Do a workout. Go for a walk. It doesn't have to be perfect. You don't need a gym membership or a plan. Just start. Stretch, lift, jog, dance — or simply walk. No fancy techniques. No overthinking. Just move.

As you do, look around. Really look. Notice the stillness of the trees, the rhythm of your own breath, the sky above you, and the life around you. You'll begin to notice the quiet kind of beauty that exists beyond your stress — the small details we so often miss. You'll also notice something else: the world is full of people just like you, carrying invisible weights.

Yes, people are struggling — everywhere. That man rushing past you with furrowed brows, the woman waiting for the bus with tired shoulders, the delivery boy on the bike with eyes that say he hasn't rested — each one is going through something. And still, they show up. So do you. And there's something deeply healing in recognizing that simple truth: *You are not alone.*

When you move — whether through a workout that makes you sweat or a quiet walk that lets you breathe — you begin to *clean your inner world.* Not by numbing the stress, not by avoiding it, but by creating space within it. You shake loose what's stuck. You come back to your body. You reconnect with the present. Science backs this up. Movement releases endorphins, boosts dopamine, balances cortisol.

Whether it's a 20-minute stretch or a fast-paced walk, physical activity clears the fog and restores your sense of control. You feel more grounded, less trapped.

And remember: you don't need to perform. You just need to *move*. Not to escape — but to *release*. This is how stress becomes manageable: not by suppressing it, but by channeling it out of your system, one breath and one step at a time.

5. CULTIVATING EMOTIONAL INTELLIGENCE

- Understand Your Emotional Patterns
- Build Empathy Without Losing Boundaries
- Navigate Difficult Conversations Calmly
- Practice Active Listening

UNDERSTAND YOUR EMOTIONAL PATTERNS

We often imagine emotions as fleeting states—temporary clouds drifting through our minds. But the truth is more intricate. Emotions are not random; they follow patterns. These emotional patterns silently shape our behaviors, our pace, our thoughts, and even our identity. Like invisible scripts, they run beneath the surface of daily life—predictable, automatic, and often unconscious. Until we pause and look within, these patterns will quietly steer our lives, creating emotional loops that feel familiar but leave us feeling stuck.

You might think you're simply reacting to the moment, but many of your responses are echoes of old experiences. An anxious thought before a challenge may not be about the present at all—it might be the voice of a younger self who once felt incapable. That sharp flash of anger might be less about the comment made today, and more about an unmet need from years ago. Emotional patterns aren't just feelings; they're coded with memory, habit, identity, and survival. They become the lens through which we interpret life. And without awareness, they trap us in repetitive emotional cycles that drain our energy and distort our clarity.

Most people live *inside* their emotional patterns without realizing it. When overwhelmed, they retreat. When criticized, they shut down. When afraid, they procrastinate. Emotional reactivity becomes a silent thief—it steals time, and decision-making power.

Those who are overly entangled in their emotional landscape often delay actions, overanalyze simple choices, and stay in cycles of guilt, fear, or doubt. Meanwhile, those who develop awareness of their emotional responses tend to move faster and with more precision—not because they feel less, but because they *understand more*. They have created space between emotion and action.

When you begin to master your emotions, an inner transformation takes root. You stop absorbing every reaction as a reflection of your worth. The raised eyebrow, the sharp tone, the unexpected silence—none of it pierces you the way it once did. Because now, you understand: most emotional exchanges are not personal assaults, but projections of others' inner storms. This realization liberates you. It gives you the power to stay anchored, calm, and present even when the world around you feels emotionally charged.

This grounded presence reshapes the way you listen. You begin to notice the fear behind the frustration, the hurt behind the harshness, the unspoken need beneath the silence. This is empathy in its truest form. You stop listening to respond and start listening to understand. Your attention becomes a sanctuary, and others feel seen in your presence—not judged, not analyzed, just seen.

This is why emotional mastery is the invisible architecture of extraordinary communication and leadership. It doesn't shout.

It doesn't demand. But its impact is undeniable. It builds trust without needing approval, connection without clinging, and depth without drama. It allows you to lead not with dominance, but with presence. To inspire not through pressure, but through example. And in this quiet power, people feel safe, understood, and moved—not because you controlled the conversation, but because you elevated it.

But none of this happens without discipline. Emotional strength is trained like a muscle. You must practice again and again: catching yourself before the spiral, choosing presence over panic, curiosity over judgment. You must choose to pause, to breathe, to reflect—not because it's easy, but because it's freeing. And with every conscious choice, you expand the space between stimulus and response. In that space, you create your life with clarity instead of chaos.

In the end, to understand your emotional patterns is to reclaim authorship of your inner world. No longer tossed by the winds of moods or triggers, you become deeply rooted in self-knowledge. You don't have to fix every emotion—but you must *face* them. And as you do, you discover something remarkable: your emotions were never the enemy. They were always the guide.

Emotional mastery begins with awareness—but awareness alone isn't enough. We must take conscious steps to *shift* our emotional patterns. This doesn't mean becoming emotionally perfect. It means becoming emotionally *curious, conscious,* and *deliberate*.

The following practices are simple yet powerful steps that gradually refine your mindset and emotional response."

1. Notice Your Triggers

Every emotional pattern has a starting point—a trigger that pulls you into a familiar loop. Begin to observe what sets your emotions ablaze. Is it criticism? Being ignored? Feeling rushed? When someone doesn't reply? These aren't just irritations; they're doorways into deeper emotional stories. The moment you identify your triggers, you start seeing your emotional foundation with greater accuracy. This awareness is the first step in rewriting it.

2. Replace Judgment with Questions

One of the fastest ways to shift an emotional pattern is to question it—gently. When you feel upset, frustrated, or overwhelmed, don't jump to conclusions. Instead, pause and ask: *What exactly am I feeling? What story am I telling myself right now? Is this true—or just familiar?* Questions invite introspection. They soften emotional charge and replace knee-jerk reactions with thoughtful reflection. Over time, you'll discover that most emotional spirals are rooted in unexamined assumptions. Inquiry breaks the spell.

3. Practice Daily Perspective-Shifting

Your brain is wired to notice threats more than blessings—it's how we survived as a species. But emotional mastery rewires that instinct. One of the simplest ways to shift your emotional baseline is to end each day by naming three things that went well. These don't have to be major victories—just moments of peace, effort, or beauty. This act trains your mind to seek what's working instead of spiraling into what's lacking.

Practicing this like: Keep a "Wins and Wonders" notebook. Every night, write down three good things about the day. Over time, this cultivates a gratitude-based emotional lens that steadies you even when challenges come.

4. Name Your Values in Difficult Moments

5. When emotions run high, it's easy to get swept into reaction—say what you don't mean, withdraw, or become defensive. In these moments, stop and ground yourself in your core values. Ask: *What would integrity choose here? What does my highest self want to do—not just my most hurt self?* Values create a stable foundation when emotions shake the ground beneath you. They offer direction when confusion clouds your path.

6. Celebrate Without Hesitation

Many people have unknowingly trained themselves to postpone joy. They believe celebration must be earned with exhaustion, success, or perfection. But this mindset diminishes your emotional vitality. Joy isn't a distraction from seriousness—it is a source of strength. When you honor the small wins, the daily efforts, the simple blessings, you nourish your resilience.

Emotional health is built in moments of gratitude and celebration.

Understanding your emotional patterns isn't a one-time revelation. It's a lifelong practice of noticing, pausing, reflecting, and reorienting. The more you engage with these habits, the more empowered you become—not to control your emotions, but to conduct them with grace. You are not meant to be a passive responder in the theater of your inner world. You are meant to be its composer.

Mastering your emotions is not about being perfect; it's about choosing, every day, to show up for yourself with courage and kindness. Lead your inner world well, and no challenge will be too great."

BUILD EMPATHY WITHOUT LOSING BOUNDARIES

Empathy is not an accessory emotion. It is one of the highest forms of human intelligence — the ability to emotionally tune in, to sense the heartbeat of someone else's experience, and to genuinely *connect*. We often speak of intelligence as logic, speed, or achievement. But to be empathetic — to feel with someone, not just for them — is a mastery that goes beyond intellect. It's the quiet force behind trust, healing, and meaningful relationships.

And yet, empathy in its rawest, unchecked form can become something else entirely: exhaustion. Emotional burnout. Even resentment. That's not because empathy is flawed — it's because empathy without boundaries becomes unsustainable.

Let's get something very clear: empathy without limits is not compassion. It's overextension. It's depletion. It's the slow unraveling of your energy in the name of being "there" for others — until, eventually, you are no longer there for yourself.

To truly practice meaningful empathy, you need to anchor it with one essential life skill: the ability to set boundaries. Because empathy is not about giving *everything* — it's about giving wisely. The aim is not to care less. The aim is to care better.

This is where the shift happens — when empathy becomes mature, intentional, and lasting. It moves from being reactive and draining, to being aware and conscious. You're still showing up. You're still listening. You're still holding space for others. But you're doing so without sacrificing your peace or identity in the process.

Think for a moment about someone you know — or perhaps someone you've seen — who embodies this kind of grounded empathy. They listen with full presence. They validate others' experiences without trying to fix or control them. They offer support that feels steady, not scattered. And most importantly, they don't dissolve into the pain they're witnessing. They remain rooted. Clear. Centered. Their empathy is not emotional entanglement — it's emotional availability with discernment.

What sets these people apart is not their lack of feeling, but their ability to regulate it. This ability to balance presence with personal boundaries is a hallmark of emotional intelligence. Studies in psychology and neuroscience repeatedly confirm that people who develop this regulation — this self-awareness — tend to thrive in both relationships and leadership. Why? Because they know how to give without breaking. They know when to speak up, when to pause, when to support, and when to say, "This isn't mine to carry."

This is a powerful realization: **boundaries do not make you colder. They make you clearer.** They do not shut people out. They let people in — without costing you your balance. A person with boundaries can walk beside someone in pain and say, *"I care for you deeply, and I will support you — but I will not lose myself in the process."* That is empathy with integrity. That is sustainable care.

Here's the heart of it: boundaries are not walls — they are filters. They help you discern what belongs to you and what does not. When you understand that, your emotional presence becomes sharper, not duller. You stop trying to rescue people from their own growth and begin standing beside them, offering strength instead of solutions. You stop equating love with sacrifice, and start practicing love with self-respect.

And that's the kind of empathy the world needs more of — not the kind that burns you out, but the kind that fuels connection *without compromising your inner ground.*

So if you've ever found yourself emotionally exhausted from caring too much, or feeling guilty for needing space, know this: empathy and boundaries are not opposites. They are partners. One allows you to feel. The other allows you to keep feeling without falling apart.

This is how empathy becomes not just a beautiful trait — but a lifelong strength. Let's look at the contrast:

Unfiltered empathy can show up as:

- Absorbing others' emotions
- Feeling responsible for others' happiness
- Saying yes when you mean no
- Burning out from over-caring
- Avoiding conflict to maintain peace
- Losing touch with your own needs

Empathy with boundaries looks like:

- Holding space without absorbing pain
- Listening without fixing
- Being kind without overextending
- Saying no with clarity and warmth
- Offering support without losing self-respect
- Recognizing your limits and honoring them

The key here is presence. When you show up for others while remaining fully present with yourself, you offer something rare — connection without codependence. You can say, *"I understand that you're hurting, and I care deeply,"* and still add, *"But I cannot sacrifice my well-being to carry it for you."* This isn't selfish — it's self-respect.

Empathy is not the act of shrinking yourself to ease someone else's discomfort. It is not about dimming your light so others can shine, nor about forfeiting your needs to cushion someone else's crisis. True empathy begins when you are so deeply anchored in your own sense of self — your values, emotions, and boundaries — that you can fully witness another person's experience without the compulsion to fix, absorb, or control it.

Real empathy doesn't create pressure. It creates space. The space to be seen. The space to feel. The space to process — without judgment, without demands, and without entanglement. And yet, this space is not built overnight. It is a skill — a delicate balance — that requires ongoing practice.

You begin by listening to your body. When a conversation feels heavy or your emotional

reserves start to thin, you pause. You don't push through with performative care. You check in. You ask: *Am I offering genuine support, or am I stepping into a role that isn't mine to play? Am I connecting or rescuing?* These reflections aren't selfish — they're signs of emotional integrity.

With time, you become more honest about your boundaries. Not to retreat or disconnect, but so you can continue showing up — *fully, authentically, sustainably.* You stop overcommitting. You stop internalizing others' chaos. And instead, you lead with grounded presence and energy that's generous but not depleting.

So when people say, *"Don't lose yourself,"* this is what they mean. Let your heart be open — empathetic, soft, receptive — but let your spine stay strong. You can be both tender and unwavering. Both compassionate and clear. Emotional clarity doesn't oppose empathy — it empowers it. It gives empathy the structure it needs to endure.

KEEP THIS IN MIND,

- Empathy and boundaries are not opposing forces — they are two sides of emotional maturity. Together, they allow you to care without collapsing.
- Emotional presence doesn't mean emotional absorption. You can support someone deeply without taking on their emotional burden.
- Setting a boundary is not a rejection — it's a form of self-alignment. It teaches people how to relate to you with respect.
- You are allowed to say, *"I care about you, and this is what I can offer right now."* That's what sustainable compassion sounds like.

Empathy without boundaries burns out. Empathy with boundaries builds connection, clarity, and mutual respect.

NAVIGATE DIFFICULT CONVERSATIONS CALMLY

There's a point in every meaningful life where we must stop protecting others' comfort at the expense of our truth. Difficult conversations are unavoidable — not because we seek conflict, but because truth eventually becomes too heavy to keep inside. These moments are not just about communication; they are thresholds. They define the line between who you've been and who you're becoming. And if you want peace, growth, and real connection, you must learn how to speak with both honesty and grace — especially when it's hard.

Too many of us carry around unspoken resentments, walking through life like emotional time bombs, all because we've been taught that peace means silence. But peace without truth is not peace — it's suppression. Avoiding a difficult conversation might make today easier, but it builds walls for tomorrow. When you suppress your truth to keep the surface calm, you trade long-term clarity for short-term comfort. And that cost is too high. Because eventually, that silence will turn into distance — from others, and from yourself.

To navigate tough conversations calmly, you must first reframe what "calm" truly means. Calm is not passive. It's not avoidance. It's not smiling through gritted teeth or pretending everything's fine. Real calm is clarity. It is the ability to sit in discomfort without rushing to escape it. It's the decision to respond rather than react. When you are calm, you're not shutting down your emotions — you're guiding them. You're present enough to speak truthfully without letting fear hijack your voice.

And here's the thing most people forget: calm communication begins long before the words are spoken. It starts with self-awareness. Before entering any challenging conversation, ask yourself, *What am I feeling? What am I afraid of? What do I truly want from this?* These questions are not soft. They are powerful. They turn emotional chaos into inner clarity — and clarity is what makes your voice steady, your message clear, and your presence unshakable.

You'll know you've grown when you can say hard things with an open heart. Not to wound, not to control, but to connect. It may sound like, *"This is hard for me to say, but it's important,"* or *"I care about this relationship, and that's why I want to be honest."* These statements disarm defensiveness and create space for vulnerability. When you speak from ownership instead of blame, from truth instead of tension, even the most difficult conversations become opportunities

— for healing, understanding, and growth.

Of course, not everyone will meet your calm with grace. Some will deflect, deny, or project. That's okay. Their reaction is not your responsibility. Your only job is to stay rooted in your truth, not to convince or please. Boundaries will be tested. Emotions may flare. But if you hold your center, if you remember who you are and what you're here to say, you stay in your power. Calm is not a performance — it's a practice. It's choosing to stay anchored even when the waters rise.

People often mistake calm for weakness, but nothing could be further from the truth. It takes immense strength to pause, to breathe, and to choose truth over reaction. It takes emotional intelligence to remain steady when old habits beg you to shout, retreat, or explode. Calm doesn't mean the conversation won't be hard — it means *you* won't be hijacked by it. You hold space for the other person, yes — but also for yourself. You remember that your needs, feelings, and boundaries are valid, even if they're hard for someone else to hear.

When you make this a way of life — when you consistently approach conflict with calm truth — everything changes. You stop being afraid of confrontation. You stop shrinking to be liked. You stop carrying conversations that were never yours to begin with. And you start building relationships where truth is welcome, where connection is real, and where emotional safety is mutual. This is where peace lives — not in silence, but in courage.

If you've been walking on eggshells, overexplaining yourself, or staying quiet just to keep others comfortable, it's time to shift. It's time to choose truth over tension. And yes, it will take courage. But that courage will give you something far greater than approval — it will give you self-respect. The kind that says, *"I will no longer abandon myself to be accepted."* That's when your voice becomes powerful. That's when calm becomes your strength.

REMEMBER THIS

- Difficult conversations aren't about winning — they're about being real.
- Avoiding discomfort creates emotional distance; facing it builds trust and clarity.
- Calm doesn't mean silence — it means speaking with self-control, not self-abandonment.
- You don't need to overexplain, convince, or fix — just express your truth with care.
- Boundaries during hard conversations are not rejection; they are self-respect in action.
- When you stay rooted in your truth, others' reactions stop controlling your peace.
- Honest communication invites growth — for you and the relationship.
- You don't have to shout to be heard. Calm truth is louder than defensiveness.
- The ability to speak clearly, kindly, and firmly is a sign of emotional maturity.
- When you change how you speak, you don't just change the conversation — you often transform yourself.

PRACTICE ACTIVE LISTENING

IN ORDER TO BE A GOOD SPEAKER, YOU SHOULD BE A GOOD LISTERNER

The Transformative Power of Active Listening

1. **Gains Trust and Genuine Respect**

When you listen attentively without interrupting, people recognize your composure, emotional maturity, and depth. This earns their respect naturally — no demand required.

2. **Deepens Personal and Professional Bonds**

Authentic listening fosters real connection. Whether at home or in the office, people are drawn to those who make them feel truly heard and understood.

3. **Amplifies Your Leadership Presence**

Those who lead by listening are perceived as thoughtful, fair, and empowering. Valuing others' voices enhances your authority and positions you as a respected leader.

4. **Minimizes Misunderstandings and Conflict**

Careful listening helps you catch potential issues before they turn into problems. It keeps conversations clear, calm, and productive.

5. **Sharpens Your Ability to Solve Problems**

Listening deeply reveals what's really going on beneath the surface, enabling you to approach problems with precision and insight.

6. **Strengthens Your Professional Reputation**

Professionals who listen with intention and clarity are recognized as respectful, composed, and highly reliable — the kind of people others look up to and count on.

6. LEADING WITH A STRONG MIND

- Set Clear Personal Boundaries
- Align Actions With Core Values
- Inspire Through Consistent Integrity
- Build Trust Through Authenticity

SET CLEAR PERSONAL BOUNDARIES

What Boundaries Really Are

Boundaries are not about shutting people out—they're about letting yourself in.

At their essence, personal boundaries are the invisible structures we create to protect our emotional, physical, mental, and spiritual well-being. Think of them not as prison walls, but as the carefully drawn lines on a map that help you navigate your own life terrain with awareness and intention. Boundaries don't say, *"Stay away."* They say, *"Here's how I can be approached."*

They communicate what is acceptable to you and what is not—what you will allow into your world, and what you will no longer entertain. They answer critical, soul-honoring questions:

What do I need to feel safe, respected, and whole? Where am I compromising too much?

What kind of relationships do I truly want to build?

To live without boundaries is to live in a state of emotional confusion. Without them, we often find ourselves saying yes when we mean no, offering time we don't have, agreeing to things that silently erode our joy. We act not out of alignment, but out of guilt, obligation, or fear—fear of disappointing others, fear of seeming selfish, fear of rejection.

But when you establish healthy boundaries, a shift occurs. You begin to act from your *center*, not your chaos. You stop being reactive and start being responsive. You speak your truth—not with anger or resentment, but with firmness and self-respect. Boundaries become your inner compass, pointing you toward decisions that reflect your values and uphold your dignity.

Let's use a metaphor that makes this concept vivid: imagine your life as a home. Your inner world is the space you've worked hard to build—it holds your values, your energy, your dreams, and your emotional well-being. Now, picture living in that home with every door and window left open, day and night. Strangers walk in without knocking. Some bring in dirt. Others rearrange your furniture or take things without asking. Slowly, your space begins to feel foreign to you. Messy. Unsafe. Disrespected.

That's what life feels like without boundaries.

But when you begin setting boundaries, it's as if you install a sturdy but welcoming fence. You decide who enters, when they enter, and how they behave when they're inside. You still host guests. You still show love. But you do so on terms that honor both your space and theirs.

Self-defined lines don't block love—they define its healthy flow.

They teach others how to treat you. But more importantly, they teach *you* how to treat *yourself.* Every boundary you set says, *I am worthy of protection. I am deserving of peace. I will no longer betray myself for the comfort of others.*

Why We Avoid Setting Them

Despite how essential boundaries are, the irony is this: many of us avoid setting them—not because we don't want to, but because we're afraid of what setting them might cost.

Let's be honest: boundaries challenge two deeply rooted fears—**the fear of confrontation and the fear of not being enough**.

It can feel deeply uncomfortable to say no. Especially if you've spent your life equating kindness with compliance. If you've been raised in environments—family, schools, relationships—where love had to be earned by sacrifice, where your voice was minimized, or where saying "no" came with consequences, then boundaries will feel unnatural at first. Even wrong.

Many of us were silently taught that to be good means to be agreeable. That to be liked, we must always be available. That to keep the peace, we must avoid rocking the boat. So we shrink ourselves, silence our needs, and accommodate others at the cost of our own emotional bandwidth.

But here's the painful truth: goodness that comes at the expense of your mental well-being is not goodness—it's self-abandonment.

Personal limits are not about becoming cold or selfish. They are about becoming **clear and courageous**.

Because setting a boundary means choosing yourself. It means standing up for your truth even if it makes others uncomfortable. It means honoring your energy even if it means someone else is inconvenienced. It means saying, *"I matter too."*

And that takes courage.

It takes courage to disappoint others so you don't disappoint yourself. It takes courage to say "no" without explanation.

It takes courage to believe that you are worthy of emotional safety.

But with every boundary you set, your self-respect deepens. Your confidence grows. And slowly, you create a life that feels like your own—one where peace is not a rare exception, but your daily standard.

Your inner wisdom already knows. All it needs is your permission to protect you.

The Empowered Shift

Something transformative begins to unfold the moment you start honoring your personal limits. You stop living in constant reaction to others. The quiet resentment that once simmered beneath the surface begins to fade. And for the first time, you feel no compulsion to justify your choices or over-explain your truth. You begin to move through life with clarity and purpose.

You come to understand that it's more than acceptable—it's *necessary*—to say:

- "Now isn't a good time for me."
- "That doesn't align with what I need."

"I value this relationship, but I need space to breathe."

And when you speak these words, something powerful shifts within you. Your posture changes—not just physically, but emotionally. You stop contorting yourself to meet the expectations of others. You stop shrinking to accommodate spaces that were never meant to contain you.

Instead of showing up solely as a fixer, a giver, or a peacekeeper—you begin to show up as *you.* Fully. Honestly. Unapologetically.

Let this be your reminder: setting a boundary is not about pushing others away—it's about

drawing yourself closer to your center. It's not an act of separation. It's an act of self-devotion.

You were never meant to be everything for everyone. You were meant to be whole.

"A boundary is a promise made in clarity. It says: I know who I am, I know what I value, and I choose to honor that even when it's hard. True strength is not in how much you endure, but in how clearly you define what you will no longer carry."

ALIGN ACTIONS WITH CORE VALUES

In a world of constant noise and endless options, the most powerful thing you can do is act in alignment with your core values. When your actions reflect your deepest beliefs, something extraordinary happens: you begin to feel whole. You stop performing for approval and start living with integrity.

Core values are not abstract ideas tucked away in the corners of self-help books. They are the emotional and ethical compass that quietly guides your choices when no one is watching.

Honesty. Compassion. Growth. Loyalty. Freedom. Discipline. Love. These are not just words — they are commitments that define how you show up in the world.

But here's the tension: we often *know* our values, yet act in ways that contradict them. We value peace but participate in drama. We value truth but avoid hard conversations. We value growth but choose comfort. This misalignment may not cause an earthquake, but it creates small fractures within — tiny betrayals that add up over time and leave us feeling disconnected, unfulfilled, or restless.

The journey of alignment begins with awareness. Ask yourself: *What truly matters to me? What are the non-negotiables in my life? What am I unwilling to compromise, even when it's inconvenient or unpopular?* Your answers become your anchor.

Once you're clear, the real work begins — translating those values into action. If you value integrity, you speak the truth even when your voice shakes. If you value compassion, you lead with empathy even when others are unkind. If you value discipline, you show up even when motivation runs dry. That is alignment: living in a way where your words, decisions, and energy reflect your inner code.

You will not always get it right. But every time you choose to realign — to recalibrate your behavior toward your beliefs — you build self-trust. And self-trust is the foundation of confidence, purpose, and peace

Alignment doesn't mean life gets easier. It means life gets clearer. You waste less energy pretending, defending, or explaining. You begin to lead yourself with quiet conviction, knowing that your life is built not on reactions, but on values that endure.

In the end, the most magnetic people, the most fulfilled lives, and the most lasting impact don't come from talent alone — they come from a consistent, courageous decision to let values lead the way

Living Authentically in Public and Private

Authentic living does not promise applause. In fact, it often disappoints those who benefitted from your performance. But it offers you something greater: the ability to look in the mirror and know that what you see is real. The ability to go to sleep with a calm heart, not because everything is easy, but because everything is true.

When your inner and outer worlds match — when your values show up in your choices, not just in your words — you become trustworthy, not just to others, but to yourself. And that trust becomes your compass. It guides your decisions, anchors your relationships, and quiets the chaos of comparison.

To live authentically in both public and private is a form of spiritual clarity. It is the quiet revolution of the soul, no longer seeking to be approved, but simply to be whole.

Living as a Daily Act of Alignment

There is a quiet dignity in choosing alignment every single day — not as a grand declaration, but as a simple, consistent practice. Most people imagine alignment as a dramatic transformation, a life-altering epiphany that suddenly sets everything right. But in truth, alignment is far less theatrical. It is gentle. It is ordinary. It is found in the tiny moments where you honor what you believe, even when no one else sees it.

You choose not to gossip, not because you want to appear noble, but because you value respect. You leave a conversation that feels misaligned, not out of arrogance, but because you protect your peace. You say no when something compromises your well-being, even if it costs you approval. These are not glamorous acts. But they are sacred ones.

The most aligned lives are deeply rooted in purpose. You feel it in how a person carries themselves — a softness, a clarity, a confidence. People like this don't have to prove who they are, because their lives already speak for them.

Daily alignment is a practice. It is waking up and choosing again to walk in integrity, even if yesterday you stumbled. It is recognizing when you're off course and gently bringing yourself back without distractions. It is forgiving yourself quickly so you can return to truth without delay.

It is also deeply personal. What alignment looks like for one person may not look the same for another. That's because it's not about what others expect — it's about what resonates with your inner compass. And the more you act from that place, the stronger your self-trust becomes.

You begin to move through the world less influenced by noise and more attuned to what feels right in your bones. .

Living in alignment is not a final destination. It's a way of being — a devotion, a discipline, a sacred rhythm you return to, day after day.

And over time, this daily practice of honoring what you value becomes not just a habit, but a way of life. A life that reflects who you truly are — not just in your words, but in the quiet, unwavering choices you make when no one is watching.

INSPIRE THROUGH CONSISTENT INTEGRITY

True leadership is never about titles. It's about trust. And trust isn't built in a day — it's built in the quiet, unshakeable repetition of integrity. Not once. Not twice. But day after day, choice after choice, especially when it's hard, inconvenient, or unnoticed.

To inspire others, you don't need to be perfect — you need to be consistent. And nothing is more consistent than integrity. It is the internal compass that quietly guides you when the crowd is loud. It's the decision to be honest when a lie would be easier, to uphold your word even when no one is checking, and to lead with values instead of ego.

There's a story I carry with me, one I heard from a retired army general who once led thousands of soldiers. He said the most important moment of his career wasn't on a battlefield, in a briefing room, or at a press conference. It was in a storm — literal and figurative — when a supply truck broke down, and his team was stranded for hours in freezing rain. Instead of staying in the vehicle, he stepped out and stood in the cold with his men. He didn't say much. He just stood there — soaked, silent, shivering — until another truck arrived.

When asked why, he simply said, *"If I'm asking them to endure something, I should be willing to endure it too."* That moment stayed with his troops for decades. Not because of a motivational speech. But because of presence. Because of integrity in action.

That is leadership. That is inspiration.

People don't remember everything you say But, Your integrity — how you treat people when it's not required, how you carry yourself when no one is watching — becomes the message you give to the world. It tells others, *This is what's possible when you don't compromise who you are to get ahead.*

You inspire not by pointing the way, but by walking it. You model a standard — through example. And in doing so, you give others permission to rise, not out of fear, but out of

reverence for what's right.

Consistent integrity also frees you. You don't have to remember who you were in different rooms, or shift to fit new opinions. You become anchored — unshaken by applause or criticism. Because your compass doesn't change with the weather.

That steadiness, that rootedness, becomes a lighthouse for others. In a world full of mixed signals and moral shortcuts, people are drawn to what's unwavering. And your integrity

— lived out not in moments of ease, but in trials of choice — becomes your greatest influence.

Not every leader inspires. But every person who leads with integrity inevitably does.

BUILD TRUST THROUGH AUTHENTICITY

As you reach the final pages of this journey, let this truth anchor within you: trust blossoms from honesty, presence, and unwavering consistency. At the heart of every grounded and resilient mind lives a quiet devotion to authenticity. And from that place of truthfulness, lasting trust naturally rises.

This is how strong minds work. Quietly. Boldly. Authentically.

Their presence offers calm, their choices radiate wisdom, and their words reflect alignment between thought, emotion, and action.

True influence emerges from realness. People are drawn to those who embody their values, express their intentions with clarity, and walk their path with courage. When your inner world is in harmony with your outer presence, you become a beacon of steadiness — someone others feel safe beside, someone who uplifts by simply being whole.

As you step forward, carry this awareness:

You are filled with remarkable calm, clarity, and conviction. With a mind that honors truth and a heart that stays open, trust flows with ease. Live each day with intention. Lead with compassion. Let your inner radiance shine — not to control, but to elevate. The most powerful minds create harmony. They reflect peace wherever they go.

Speak this to yourself — not as a wish, but as your truth:

I am confident. I am powerful.

My strength rises from the peace I have made within myself. I recognize my voice as meaningful and my path as worthy. I move forward with grace, choosing depth over noise, presence over pressure.

I trust the clarity of my thoughts. I embrace the wisdom of my emotions. I grow with purpose, choosing stillness when others rush, choosing awareness where others drift.

My worth is evident in how I show up. My belief in myself lights every room I enter. Each step I take now reflects intention, alignment, and quiet courage.

I rise with purpose. I create impact through presence. And I lead with a heart that stays open, steady, and true.